Primary Schools and Special Needs: Policy, Planning and Provision

Sheila Wolfendale

Cassell

Cassell Educational Limited
Artillery House
Artillery Row
London SW1P 1RT

British Library Cataloguing in Publication Data

Wolfendale, Sheila
   Primary schools and special needs : policy,
   planning and provision.—(Special needs
   in ordinary schools)
   1. Exceptional children—Education
   (Elementary)—Great Britain   2. Mainstreaming in education—Great Britain
   I. Title II. Series
   371.9'0941   LC3986.G7

ISBN: 0 – 304 – 31388 –2

Typeset by Activity Ltd., Salisbury, Wilts.
Printed and bound in Great Britain by
Biddles Ltd., Guildford and King's Lynn

Last digit is print no: 9 8 7 6 5 4 3 2 1

SPECIAL NEEDS IN ORDINARY SCHOOLS
General Editor: Peter Mittler

Primary Schools and Special Needs

Special Needs in Ordinary Schools

General editor: Peter Mittler
Associate editors: James Hogg, Peter Pumfrey, Tessa Roberts,
Colin Robson
Honorary advisory board: Neville Bennett, Marion Blythman,
George Cooke, John Fish, Ken Jones, Sylvia Phillips, Klaus Wedell,
Phillip Williams

Titles in this series

Meeting Special Needs in Ordinary Schools: An Overview

Concerning pre- and primary schooling:

Communication in the Primary School
Exploring the Environment
Expressive and Creative Skills
Fostering Mathematical and Scientific Thinking in Primary Schools
Primary Schools and Special Needs: Policy, Planning and Provision
Special Needs in Pre-Schools

Concerning secondary schooling:

Communication in the Secondary School
School and Beyond
Science for All: Teaching Science in the Secondary School
Secondary Schools for All? Strategies for Special Needs
*Humanities and Children with Special Educational Needs in Secondary
Schools*
Teaching Mathematics in the Secondary School

Concerning specific difficulties:

Children with Learning Difficulties
Children with Speech and Language Difficulties
Making a Difference: Teachers, Pupils and Behaviour
Physically Disabled Children
The Hearing Impaired Child
Visual Handicaps in the Classroom

Contents

Foreword: Towards education for all

AIMS

This series aims to support teachers as they respond to the challenge they face in meeting the needs of all children in their school, particularly those identified as having special educational needs.

Although there have been many useful publications in the field of special educational needs during the last decade, the distinguishing feature of the present series of volumes lies in their concern with specific areas of the curriculum in primary and secondary schools. We have tried to produce a series of conceptually coherent and professionally relevant books, each of which is concerned with ways in which children with varying levels of ability and motivation can be taught together. The books draw on the experience of practising teachers, teacher trainers and researchers and seek to provide practical guidelines on ways in which specific areas of the curriculum can be made more accessible to all children. The volumes provide many examples of curriculum adaptation, classroom activities, teacher–child interactions, as well as the mobilisation of resources inside and outside the school.

The volumes are organised largely in terms of age and subject groupings, but three 'overview' volumes have been prepared in order to provide an account of some major current issues and developments. Seamus Hegarty's *Meeting Special Needs in Ordinary Schools* gives an introduction to the field of special needs as a whole, whilst Sheila Wolfendale's *Primary Schools and Special Needs* and John Sayer's *Secondary Schools for All?* address issues more specifically concerned with primary and secondary schools respectively. We hope that curriculum specialists will find essential background and contextual material in these overview volumes.

In addition, a section of this series will be concerned with examples of obstacles to learning. All of these specific special needs can be seen on a continuum ranging from mild to severe, or from temporary and transient to long-standing or permanent. They include difficulties in learning or in adjustment and behaviour, as well as problems resulting largely from sensory or physical impairments or from difficulties of communication from whatever cause. We hope that teachers will consult the volumes in this section for guidance on working with children with specific difficulties.

The series aims to make a modest 'distance learning' contribution to meeting the needs of teachers working with the whole range of pupils with special educational needs by offering a set of resource materials relating to specific areas of the primary and secondary curriculum and by suggesting ways in which learning obstacles, whatever their origin, can be identified and addressed.

We hope that these materials will not only be used for private study but be subjected to critical scrutiny by school-based inservice groups sharing common curricular interests and by staff of institutions of higher education concerned with both special needs teaching and specific curriculum areas. The series has been planned to provide a resource for LEA advisers, specialist teachers from all sectors of the education service, educational psychologists, and teacher working parties. We hope that the books will provide a stimulus for dialogue and serve as catalysts for improved practice.

It is our hope that parents will also be encouraged to read about new ideas in teaching children with special needs so that they can be in a better position to work in partnership with teachers on the basis of an informed and critical understanding of current difficulties and developments. The goal of 'Education for All' can only be reached if we succeed in developing a working partnership between teachers, pupils, parents, and the community at large.

The publishers and I would like to thank the many people – too numerous to mention – who have helped to create this series. In particular we would like to thank the Associate Editors, James Hogg, Peter Pumfrey, Tessa Roberts and Colin Robson, for their active advice and guidance; the Honorary Advisory Board, Neville Bennett, Marion Blythman, George Cooke, John Fish, Ken Jones, Sylvia Phillips, Klaus Wedell and Phillip Williams, for their comments and suggestions; and the teachers, teacher trainers and special needs advisers who took part in our information surveys.

Professor Peter Mittler   University of Manchester
                                           January 1987

Acknowledgements

A number of people have given central or 'sidelines' support to me in writing this book. There are some to whom I particularly wish to express thanks.

To Peter Mittler and Juliet Wight-Boycott I express my appreciation for their editorial comments and encouragement. I wish to thank Julie, Ann, Lilian, and Mary in the Psychology Department at North East London Polytechnic for having been willing to type the book and who accepted, with little demur, my smuggling of each hand-written chapter into the typing tray.

Finally I want to record thanks and love to my long-suffering family, to Trevor, Daniel and Rachel who, as ever, are my mainstay.

Sheila Wolfendale
London
November 1986

To Sally and Ronald Sefton, my mother and father

Preface

The bibliography of books on 'special educational needs' is now rapidly growing. Teachers and other practitioners within education can increasingly avail themselves of practical 'tips', ideas for curriculum and classwork that are couched within or are derived from one or other theoretical framework or set of principles. Likewise, as never before in the history of 'special education' in the United Kingdom, issues are discussed to do with the integration of children, and opening up mainstream educational processes to all children.

These current debates and evolving educational practice provide the backcloth to this book. However, because it is a part of a series, it attempts both to be freestanding, of use in its own right, as well as to provide a coherent statement about special needs in primary settings that will set the scene for the books on primary matters later in the series. I draw freely upon seminal and innovative work in special needs as well as upon contemporary views on primary education, in order to make my own statement and to make my position clear.

It will be evident to those readers who pursue their path through the chapters that a certain set of educational philosophies is expounded.

Chapter 1 sets out to locate the concept of special educational needs and, whilst acknowledging the elusive and at times illusory nature of the concept, attempts an unequivocal statement about the learning and emotional needs of every child. The ideological difficulties in deriving formulae about 'special educational needs' are examined in reference to broader perspectives on primary education and with a view to some sort of synthesis.

Throughout the book the expressed commitment is towards the evolution and adoption of 'collective responsibility' for children with identified special educational needs. This encompasses, without question, the involvement and contribution of their parents and caregivers within community contexts. These dimensions are particularly addressed in chapter 2.

Chapters 3 and 4 single out two major areas of concern to many teachers and others in education, namely learning and behaviour difficulties. A balance is sought between formulating in practical terms, strategies that can be adopted to tackle identified problems whilst, at the same time, reiterating how context-specific, even relative, these issues can be. The broader, 'school as a system' context is examined in chapter 5, which also sets out the 'collective responsibility' idea in workable terms. No blueprint for educational action nowadays would be complete without discussion on staff development and support and the inservice training needs of teachers, and this is the focus of chapter 6. Since the preceding chapters provide the basis for a school policy for special educational needs, chapter 7 sets out to formulate and discuss the elements which could form such a policy. The quite explicit message is that now, in the mid 1980s, it should now be incumbent upon schools and their LEAs to have written, accountable policies.

Chapter 8 the final chapter. It is only short but it aims to provide a bridge between primary and secondary settings and discusses ways of bringing about a smooth transition for those children who may be especially vulnerable at this potentially critical time.

It is hoped that the readership of this book, and indeed of this series, will be wide. A fair amount of professional sophistication is assumed and, for readers who want back-up and confirmation of contemporary thinking and practice, a considerable number of references are provided. Chapters 3 and 4 carry the most references, for these are areas with direct implications for follow-up work. Texts relevant for further reading/practical application are asterisked.

In keeping with my own views, there is no intentionally sexist language. All allusions to children and adults are he/she, his/her, etc.

Finally, a word about children, who are, indeed, the 'subject matter' of this book. Running throughout this book is the assumption that we address ourselves to all children, irrespective of background and circumstance, yet we live in an era when, justifiably, we perceive that our professional responsibilities towards children from ethnic minority backgrounds must include action that is affirmative. At a time, that is, that the last 10 to 20 years or so have characterised for many families as one of cultural transition. We must be sensitive towards the 'distinctive needs' (Wolfendale, 1983) of a number of children whose learning needs are compounded in this era by their overwhelming need to benefit from, and be part of, an educational system that has operated for many, many years without particular regard to individuals or their cultural backgrounds.

My declared commitment is, then, to the provision of equal opportunities, and to the eradication of any unintentional educational practice that further disadvantages children who are already coming to terms with the functional use of more than one language, who are reconciling, coping with, and responding to

and religious frameworks (Houlton, 1986). These do not have to be 'problems' (which confirm the onus on the child and his/her family) but they do have to be 'issues' to be dealt with as part of collective responsibility which is a cornerstone philosophy of this book.

I go along with the basic premise contained in the Swann Report (1985) that unequivocally states that responsibility for providing equal access and opportunities, without prejudice, belongs to each and every school and educational institution within each and every local education authority. The Swann Report's conception of 'education for all' embraces what it terms 'the realities of British society now and in the future, that a variety of ethnic groups with their own distinct lifestyles and value systems will be living together' (Swann Report, page 324).

This, then, provides the broadest backcloth of all to this book.

REFERENCES

Houlton, D. (1986) *Cultural Diversity in the Primary School*. London: Batsford.

Swann, M. (Chair) (1985) *Education For All*. Report of the Committee of Inquiry into the Education of Children from Ethnic Minority Groups, London: HMSO.

Wolfendale, S. (1983) *Parental Participation in Children's Development and Education*. London: Gordon and Breach.

Reformulating special needs and realigning primary practice

This book is about attitude and action. It is for teachers and about teachers, and it has been written on behalf of children in primary schools.

Based on the notion that all children are special, it is a book that sets out to reconcile two major traditions in British education. One is the tradition of primary schooling, with its ideologies and well-attested pedagogies. The other tradition is that of special education, which, over the period of this century, has evolved its own separate identity and educational philosophy. Between these dominant traditions has been a third strand: the grey, nebulous area of remedial education, uneasily straddling these distinctive worlds of mainstream primary and special education. It has been allied more closely to mainstream whilst simultaneously deriving some of its identity from certain of the precepts and practices of special education.

The separate traditions permeate education – they are to be found in the literature, in library classifications, in inservice provision, in job titles, in educational research. A reconciliation is timely. The Warnock Committee pronounced that a meaningful distinction between remedial and special education could no longer be maintained, and this, of course, was a statement en route towards a re-affirmation of the principle of integrated and fully comprehensive education. Likewise, 11 years earlier the Plowden Committee, within its remit to consider the 'whole subject of primary education', was concerned with all children in primary schools and how their learning needs could be met.

An alignment between 'best' practice in primary and in special education is now called for. As schools embrace the equality of opportunity inherent in the anti-discriminatory educational policies espoused by a slowly increasing number of local education authorities, so the hard-won expertise in devising effective curricula in primary schools needs to be matched by and married to the equally hard-won expertise in remedial and special education.

Educational aims as propounded in textbooks, by LEAs and by

schools have represented a knitting together of the differing strands of education within an 'education for all' philosophy. The HMI discussion document *The Curriculum from 5 to 16* (DES, 1985) in acknowledging the commonality of educational aims stated:

> Whatever means a school uses to translate its aims into everyday curricular terms, and whatever means it uses to provide appropriately for pupils of different ages and abilities, broad aims ... should underlie its day-to-day work in respect of all its pupils.
> (page 3)

Beyond the rhetoric lies the task of translating aims into sound pedagogic practice that provides for the universality of all children's needs as well as for the specificity of each child's needs, and for the overwhelming majority whose paramount educational need is to be educated in local schools. This chapter is intended to provide the conceptual underpinning of an integrated approach to meeting special educational needs in primary schools, and to set the scene for subsequent chapters that explore the application of these views in practice.

EFFECTS OF THE DEBATE ON SPECIAL NEEDS

The opening sentence of this chapter referred to attitude. As schools interact with, and are a part of, their communities, it is the aspiration of those in favour of integrated education that greater tolerance and understanding of disability, 'deviance', and differing backgrounds will eventually inform and influence a wider public.

Case studies abound (Thomas, 1978; Thomas, 1982; Topliss, 1982) as to the entrenched and fearful prejudices of people towards 'difference' of any kind, yet 'difference' itself is shown, in surveys, to be discretely defined and usually relative. For example, a survey in Yorkshire into attitudes to Down's Syndrome revealed misunderstanding, even hostility, to mental handicap (Sinson, 1985). Polls on attitudes by a (largely) able-bodied public into disability (mental and physical) reported by McConkey and McCormack (1983) confirm equivocal and ambiguous attitudes; misunderstanding and sympathy co-exist uneasily. McConkey and McCormack are confident that public attitudes to, and acceptance of, disability can be altered, and their book brims with practical group and community activities designed to bring about change. Shearer (1981), too, is a writer who lays the responsibility for attitude change and proper provision for disabled persons squarely on all sectors of society.

The educational community, in part by virtue of legislative change, is charged with a particular responsibility to open the debate locally and keep it vibrant. Some local education authorities have taken this responsibility seriously and have produced consultative documents on special needs, policies and provision. The best known of these is the ILEA Fish Report (1985), which undoubtedly perceived that its remit lay within the broader context of equal and anti-discriminatory educational opportunities and that the effects of its recommendations should, therefore, be pervasive. The implications of special needs and integrationist policies within education upon society at large are clear:

> This policy should stress that the important human needs are common to all and of greater significance than the special needs associated with disabilities and difficulties. Unless and until this is recognised and accepted, those children and young people with special needs will continue to be marginalised, and efforts to achieve their integration into society will tend to remain limited.
> (Fish Report, 1985, page 6, 1.1.30)

The opening up of debate, the abolition of statutory categories of handicap, and the changed terminology do seem to be bringing about attitude change (e.g., the chronicled readiness of an increasing number of nursery, infant, and first schools to admit Down's Syndrome children). But the change in nomenclature has created a dilemma that concerns the very term 'special educational needs' (Wedell, 1983; Galloway, 1985) in the necessarily arbitrary nature of the cut-off point of 'special' (Gipps, Goldstein and Gross, 1985) and the inescapable, and not always benign, influence of social interests and vested power upon the consideration of 'special' needs (Swann, 1981; Ford, Mongon and Whelan, 1982; Barton and Tomlinson, 1984).

The paradox appears implacable – it is that there is a percentage of children who, at any one time, will be deemed to 'have' special educational needs (Warnock, 1978) a minority of whom will be accorded the 'protection of a statement' (via 1981 Education Act Section 5 assessment procedures) – but – conversely, *all* children are special (Brennan, 1982).

The humanitarian intention in singling out children who are said to be in need of special, different, extra provision is at odds with the perfidious effects of the label. Ensuring special attention for designated children means that those children are seen as representative of a type (special versus non-special needs). From that acknowledgement it is but a short step to categorising once more.

These contradictions bedevil all of us working in education and on behalf of children. On the one hand, it is vital to safeguard educational interests to ensure maximum protection of children with 'disabilities'. On the other hand, we are constrained by our basic human tendency to group and classify all manner of phenomena, including children in our charge. In common currency still are categories such as: disadvantaged; working-class; coming from an ethnic minority; maladjusted; slow learner; and so on. The point has been forcibly made by writers cited above and others that the maintenance of such descriptions ensures the perpetuation of the within child, deficit model (that is, the view that ascribes the problem to the child and not to external factors). Further, such grouping ensures that an individual child is less a unique *subject*, worthy of individual consideration, than an *object*, representative of a type or class and showing relevant characteristics. Schools are then absolved from critically reappraising conditions for learning, and the education service from rationalising provision.

Indeed, the legal process of assessing, discovering, identifying, and pronouncing a special need acute enough to warrant the 'protection of a statement' has generated a whole industry within education. Procedural manuals proliferate, and within each LEA, there is a proper, rule-bound specification for the implementation of these processes.

My interpretation of this view shows it as a rather nihilistic one, which sends the concept of special needs spiralling out of sight. But, in order for the actions with which this book is concerned to be robust and credible, these reminders of the pitfalls of grouping and labelling have had to be given. Before the discussion in this chapter moves on, the point has forcibly to be made that the term 'special educational needs' must not be used to differentiate individual children from one another nor groups from one another. It has to be used, as it was intended (Warnock, 1978), to ensure a match between the learning needs at any one time of an individual child and the best provision and resources that can be made available for that child.

TOWARDS A FRAMEWORK OF SUPPORT IN PRIMARY SCHOOLS

This section of the chapter contains the nub of the case for aligning primary and special education. It will pay attention to teacher education, the concept of learning needs, and the development of support networks within schools, and will examine the rationale of intervention. It will aim to present a view of primary education that is indivisible from, and indeed provides, the context for special provision.

One of the factors governing the temptation to group and label is an ignorance of the 'condition' that seems, at any one time, to obtain for a child, e.g., a learning difficulty, a behaviour problem, and the consequent uncertainty as to how to cope.

The Warnock Report recognised that as class teachers are so central to children's school lives, training and support should enable them to recognise individual children's learning needs and respond appropriately. An integrated and truly comprehensive system demands more of teachers, however. Here, again, is a potential dilemma. Teachers can expect chidren who hitherto have been in special schools to be in mainstream primaries, within any one of several variations of integration (Hodgson, Clunies-Ross and Hegarty, 1984). So they are expected to have some familiarity with ranges of learning difficulty (from moderate to severe); with degrees of physical and sensory handicap – and to respond sensitively. At the same time they cannot be experts on a whole variety of serious and complex disabilities that may require special aetiological knowledge as well as specific equipment and teaching methods. Likewise, teachers within the special education community have long been protective of children in their charge, and have themselves evolved specialisms in the realms of educating and caring for mildly and profoundly handicapped children. Can they, along with teachers in primary schools, be reassured that their charges' best interests are served in integrated settings?

Reform in education is not an overnight phenomenon. Where reforming measures combine legislative frameworks, shifts in resource allocation, changes in attitudes and expectation, there needs to be a phased programme towards goals specified for, and achievable at, each stage.

Teacher education is, therefore, a particular priority at the early stages of a programme. There needs to be a rapprochement between the relative teaching experience and educational knowledge of teachers from primary and from special education settings, so that each can inform and support the other. It is consistent with the intent of integration that knowledge about special needs, from mild, to moderate, to acute and medically-dependent conditions, should be made accessible to mainstream teachers. On the basis of being better informed and knowledgeable about where specialist support is available, they are then in a more secure and personally comfortable position to meet children's learning needs.

Consistent with this view that generalist primary teachers must be in receipt of special knowledge has come a spate of locally and regionally provided INSET textbooks. These argue a case for redirected teacher training, initial and inservice, for special needs (Sayer and Jones, 1985), and books and kits written for teachers about handicapping conditions and their teaching implications, which hitherto have been referenced in specialised, arcane or medical sections of libraries (Morgenstern, 1981; Male and Thompson, 1985; TIPS – Dawson, 1985; Gillham, 1986).

Jones (in Sayer and Jones eds, 1985) in discussing attitudes to disability and the requisites within teacher training for bringing about change, cautions against cosmetic approaches that duck the most fundamental requisite of all – namely, that the responsibility for ensuring that children's needs are met in schools is conjoint, collective and no longer the exclusive property of specially assigned teachers and other experts.

This theme will be elaborated and illustrated in this chapter and throughout this book.

THE NOTION OF COLLECTIVE RESPONSIBILITY

Even before, and certainly since the era, 20 years ago, that saw the publication of the Plowden Report, we have been accustomed to remedial teaching expertise growing up alongside generalist subject teaching at primary level. Children in need of remedial help have been siphoned off to units or small groups, injected with their dose of remedial reading and returned to their classes.

The relative ineffectiveness of such discrete jabs of remediation and the lack of generalisability of performance was commented on in the Bullock Report (1975), which laid down one of the rubrics of successful intervention with children's reading difficulties – namely, a language across the curriculum approach. This was one of the first calls for co-ordinated provision within schools and paved the way for a greater assumption of responsibility by other teachers who had contact with 'failing' children.

Even with a broader conception of special needs, and the gradual abandonment of the term 'remedial' in educational circles, there would be the danger that designated 'special needs teachers' (often called co-ordinators) would be regarded as the repository of responsibility as well as expertise. This book, and this series, takes a pluralist view of special needs, wherein the perception of a child's unique special need is that it merges into and is not easily separable from his or her universal needs. Not only does a separatist line militate against a 'pure' principle of integration, but, more pragmatically, the complex web of a child's needs are such that no one teacher can adequately meet them.

We have to acknowledge that to posit special needs is to have to provide for their being met in ordinary classrooms. It also follows that only a network of personnel and provision can ensure this. So we must abandon the old unitary view of teaching in primary schools, where the onus of responsibility is put personally onto individual class teachers. We have to move towards establishing within schools task-forces of teachers and others who have explicit and differential responsibility for carrying out a school's policy on special needs (see later in the chapter).

So, for class teachers, from their initial training onwards, special needs would not be viewed as something grafted onto the curriculum, tacked on for a minority of children. They would be able readily to accept that establishing classroom conditions conducive to learning by all children is central to their task. Likewise, the class teacher would be supported by other teachers, in terms of curriculum planning, co-teaching, monitoring, review, and in and out of school liaison. The structures within the school would also facilitate the carrying out of special needs policies and would enable collective responsibility to be exercised.

A corporate endeavour, too, would act in the interests of efficiency and cost effectiveness, facts of life that have to be considered and that indeed are conditions seen as compatible with the introduction of integration (Education Act 1981, s.2 (2), p. 2). It would encourage the best use of the panoply of outside school services, which exist to back up and supplement school-based provision, but which are not always readily accessible to class teachers and, moreover, threaten to reduce the responsibility that should be the schools'.

Within a broader context still, the responsibility towards effective implementation of a special needs policy has to be shared with the LEA advisory and administrative staff. The theme of a 'network of services' is explored in chapter 5.

A CHILD-CENTRED VIEW OF MEETING SPECIAL NEEDS IN THE PRIMARY SCHOOL

In her critique of developmental psychology and child-centred pedagogy, Walkerdine (in Henriques, 1984) tackles attitudes and practices that she says characterise the British primary school, which is:

> taken to be a paradigm of practice for a considerable proportion of the Western World. Here, children are to be enabled to develop at their own pace, to work individually, to be free and to grow up into rational adults.
> (page 153)

But to question the concept, as Walkerdine does, for failing, in its translation into practice, to liberate children and unshackle them from constraints in the social domain, is to presuppose that structure, organised teaching, and learning were never explicitly part of the child-centred ideology. That ideology itself has been prey to fashion; such that the learning by discovery approach was seen as all or none, despite discussions by Stones (1970) and others as to its many-faceted nature. As the Plowden Report put it, rather starkly, '"finding out" has proved to be better for children than "being told"' (1967, para. 1233, page 460).

This polarisation is also criticised by Alexander (1984), who writes:

> My argument is that the primary school's strengths in respect of climate and interpersonal relations are sometimes offset by weaknesses in respect of curriculum and pedagogy .... As ideology, child-centredness may be effective; as educational rationale it is sometimes deficient.
> (page 15)

The essence of a child-centred approach seems to have been the emphasis upon encouraging whole-child development within a 'progressive' frame (Galton, 1980) where a child was less coerced into learning than encouraged towards the learning opportunities made available. In short, it made the child the *subject* rather than the *object*, to be slotted into a pre-determined curriculum.

Suspicions about the effectiveness of such an approach, *laissez-faire* at worst, random at best and less amenable to measurement, have been fuelled by the increasing adoption, certainly in remedial and special settings, of objectives-based curricula. These are founded on the idea that it is in children's best learning interests, particularly for 'slow' learners, to be in receipt of a curriculum (for reading, spelling, handwriting, number, and language) (Cameron, 1981) that has been task-analysed. Longer-term goals and short-term targets can then be devised for a child whose entry skills are first appraised on a criterion-referenced placement (attainment) test (see chapter 3).

What is proposed at this point is a re-definition of child-centred education to take account of each child's learning needs, and acknowledge the 'special' nature of these, in so far as it becomes the collective responsibility of all in the school to ensure that these are met. That is, instead of children being perceived to 'fail' the curriculum (be behind in maths by the end of the year, have a reading age lower than chronological age, for example), a given child is enabled to reach realistic and achievable learning goals devised for (and with) that child from a rich and diverse bank of educational experiences.

So the notion of a 'remedial' approach for a particular child, where the provision (a DATAPAC programme, a peer-tutored, paired reading programme, for example) is uneasily appended to the child's other curriculum experiences, becomes superseded by a different conception.

That provision (examples given just above), which has been worked out by the team (see chapter 5) as being appropriate to meet the child's learning needs integrally, becomes part of the broader curriculum opportunity for the child, so that she or he can take maximum advantage of what is on offer within the school. How often has a 'remedial' child, a 'slow learner', been deprived of and cut-off from the rest of the peer group by virtue of reading and learning difficulties? The only match that has been made with his or her needs has been to provide a discrete remedial programme for a finite number of minutes per day, or times per week, based on the concept of 'failure'.

The need to assess a child's 'strengths and weaknesses' has been stressed in recent years, in order to

1. escape from the deficit model
2. use the strengths (learning assets) to compensate for the weaknesses (learning difficulties)
3. maintain motivation by acknowledging these strengths whilst working on the weaknesses.

However, the idea that a composite assessment of a child's strengths and weaknesses can be translated into teaching goals across the primary curriculum has not yet caught on widely in practice. As long as we maintain distinct areas of responsibility (remedial/advisory teacher and educational psychologist concerned with failure and remediation; class teacher concerned with the rest of the curriculum) we are unlikely to be able to cater adequately for the totality of a child's educational needs.

A child's learning strengths can be defined as: comprising those areas of the curriculum that the child enjoys, is motivated to attend, to participate and progress in, and to which he or she brings an appropriate learning style. These assets need to be capitalised upon, across and within each subject and curriculum area and a learning programme must be devised that embraces these areas. That is, instead of the remediation focussing upon the area of deficit, usually the evident, key areas of literacy and numeracy, the learning programme and the corresponding short and longer-term goals would be applied to all the areas of learning and experience defined as curriculum areas in the HMI discussion document *The Curriculum from 5 to 16* (DES, 1985).

That this has always intrinsically been the intention of teachers towards all children is not disputed. The challenge is that the intention can move towards action by a mandatory, within-school 'statement of needs' for each child, that is regularly reviewed. Although there have been earlier calls for providing learning objectives for 'slow-learning' children (McCreesh and Maher, 1974; Ainscow and Tweddle, 1979) these were not seen to be explicitly within a whole-school approach. More recent publications indicate that the notion of whole-school provision is beginning to be taken on board (Hinson and Hughes, 1982; Gulliford, 1985).

 What is proposed here as being consistent with a child-centred view of meeting special needs in primary settings is the idea of a *learning profile*. This would be devised for each child, based on an assessment of 'entry' skills evident at the time of assessment, matched with appropriate short and longer-term learning goals, which is regularly reviewed by key staff and parents. This formulation is explored further in chapter 3.

It is axiomatic, however, that teachers teach children, not classes, and as Hanko says (1985) 'with better understanding of children's special needs, teachers could rediscover a child's "teachable self"' (page 87). She further asserts, supporting the idea of the whole-school approach, and therefore implicitly endorsing the idea of collective responsibility discussed above, 'that specialists should act as facilitators in helping teachers to adapt the curriculum in the light of children's needs' (page 87).

One final word in this introduction to a redefinition of a child-centred view to meeting special needs, and one which is by way of a trailer to chapter 3. This refers to the place of norm-referenced assessment. Reference to the norm (via tests, checklists, and rating scales) is only applicable if it illuminates how to help a child. If it is not criterion-referenced, a test serves no function. An IQ test is a sterile measure that cannot provide indicators of the next teaching and learning goals. Even a reading age (Vincent & de la Mare, 1985) is notional. An assessment must work *for* and not *against* a child, i.e., an external yardstick should not be used as a measure of the 'success' or 'failure' of the child.

THE WIDER CONTEXT TO CHILDREN'S NEEDS

Whilst the preface to this book staked out the territory to be covered, this first chapter aspires to impart a statement of intent in respect of the concept of needs and a reformulation of this within a mainstream primary context. In the discussion on 'needs' the idea has lain embedded that it is the right of each child to have his or her learning and other needs fully met in school.

The ideology of this book embraces, however, not only the consideration of children's rights but those of teachers, parents, and other participants in educational processes. This sounds as if the remit is so broad that the focus of the message will be diffused. It will, though, be a central tenet that children's needs and their rights can be appraised by reference to adults of significance in their lives in so far as their influence impinges upon schooling.

The idea of collective responsibility has already been aired, and this is in keeping with the ecological perspectives to be discussed in chapter 2. Implicit in the effective functioning of the actors in the primary scenarios that are portrayed throughout the book are some fundamental features:

- that the actors' (for example, teachers, parents, support personnel, governors) roles, functions, and responsibilities have been properly defined, clarified, and delineated so that they are comfortable in them
- that the relationships between and amongst these principal actors have equally been delineated and made explicit, so that when it comes to the exercising of role and responsibilities to do with special needs provision, these demarcations facilitate the application of policy.

These remarks are not intended to be exhortatory. They are prompted by the wisdom of retrospect: looking back over time as an involved educationalist within remedial and special education, one cannot but be struck by the proliferation of personnel and provision that emerged in response to immediate need, rather than being planned as a longer-term, more measured and considered response to anticipated problems or articulated educational philosophies.

We have enough accumulated knowledge and expertise, both within primary and remedial/special settings to be able, now, to plan provision and training that incorporate adequate consideration of job satisfaction for all parties. So, in this book, attention will be paid to the professional needs of teachers and others who contribute to the life of schools. This includes consideration, too, of the self-determination of children in being involved in setting their own learning goals, and self-appraisal and self-management by teachers. Braun and Lasher (1978) refer to the role definition that is needed when 'mainstreaming' children with special needs, and Campbell (1985), within the context of British primary education, makes a case for the evolution of the 'collegial' primary school. These juxtapositions, reflecting the rapprochement called for at the beginning of this chapter, are picked up later in the book.

RATIONALE FOR INTERVENTION

Intervention in children's learning is usually perceived to be the provision of something over, above, and additional to the curriculum, and as epitomised by programme, kits, and 'packages' that have come to be associated with remedial approaches to the 'slow learner', the 'retarded', the 'underachiever'. The definition of 'intervention' by Anderson (quoted in Wolfendale and Bryans, 1979) is compatible with the idea of providing something additional to, or parallel with, the main curriculum, but could also be seen to apply to education itself. The definition given by Anderson is that intervention is 'a conscious and purposeful set of actions intended to change or influence the anticipated course of development' (Wolfendale and Bryans, 1979, page 18).

In that book we attempt to demonstrate how learning difficulties can be identified early on, and suggest lines of action both centred within the mainstream curriculum for infant and lower junior classes, as well as being additional to that curriculum. We did not wish to perpetuate the idea of a rigid distinction between a core curriculum applicable to all children and a separate, remedial provision available to some. Whilst the idea of differential teaching input must remain as being in children's best interests we are moving towards a view that an increasing number of the erstwhile-labelled 'remedial' children ought to be enabled to achieve more from the regular curriculum, whilst children with especial problems, e.g., sensory or physical difficulties can be supported to maintain close access to the curriculum.

Indeed, I (Wolfendale, 1983) have examined a rationale of intervention for all children, meaning, in the views of Shipman (1979) and Caldwell (1975) identifying the requisites for optimal learning by all children and organising the learning environment accordingly. On the premise that much learning is incidental, and that the match between teaching input and learning output (children's performance) is imperfectly understood, intervention is perceived as an intentional teaching and learning programme comprising goals, the achievement of which can be measured. This view of curriculum planning is consistent with the child-centred view of meeting children's needs described above. In this conception the distinction between remedial and non-remedial is blurred if not abolished, as intervention becomes education for all children.

Bloom (1979) went further to posit how teachers and researchers in education can positively engineer and organise the curriculum and the learning environment so as to enable virtually all students to learn to a high standard (page 1). His confident enumeration of 'alterable variables' is examined in chapter 3.

REFERENCES

Ainscow, M. and Tweddle, D. (1979) *Preventing Classroom Failure*. Chichester: Wiley.

Alexander, R. (1984) *Primary Teaching*. London: Holt Rinehart and Winston.

Barton, L. and Tomlinson, S. (eds) (1984) *Special Education and Social Interests*. London: Croom Helm.

Bloom, B. (1979) *Alterable Variables: The New Direction in Educational Research*. Edinburgh: Scottish Council for Research in Education.

Braun, S. and Lasher, M. (1978) *Are You Ready to Mainstream?* London: Charles E. Merrill.

Brennan, W. (1982) *Changing Special Education*. Milton Keynes: Open University Press.

Bullock, Lord A. (Chairman) (1975) *A Language for Life*. London: HMSO.

Caldwell, C. (1975) 'What is the optimal learning environment for the young child?' Chapter 11 in J. Sants and H. J. Butcher (eds) *Developmental Psychology*. Harmondsworth: Penguin.

Cameron, R. J. (ed.) (1981) Curriculum development, curriculum objectives issue, *Journal of Remedial Education*, **16** (4) November.

Campbell, R. J. (1985) *Developing the Primary School Curriculum*. Eastbourne: Holt, Rinehart and Winston.

Dawson, R. (1985) *TIPS, Teacher Information Packs*. Basingstoke: Macmillan.

DES (1985) *The Curriculum from 5–16: An HMI Discussion Document*. London: HMSO.

Dessent, A. (1983) Who is responsible for children with special needs? Chapter 6 in T. Booth and P. Potts *Integrating Special Education*. Oxford: Basil Blackwell.

Education Act 1981. London: HMSO.

Fish, J. (Chair) (1985) *Educational Opportunities for All?* Report of the Committee reviewing provision to meet special educational needs. London: Inner London Education Authority.

Ford, J., Mongon, D. and Whelan, M. (1982) *Special Education and Social Control*. London: Routledge and Kegan Paul.

Galloway, D. (1985) *Schools, Pupils and Special Educational Needs*. London: Croom Helm.

Galton, M., Simon, B. and Croll, P. (1980) *Inside the Primary Classroom*. London: Routledge and Kegan Paul.

Gillham, B. (ed.) (1986) *Handicapping Conditions in Children*. London: Croom Helm.

Gipps, C., Goldstein, H. and Gross, H. (1985) Twenty per cent with special needs: another legacy from Cyril Burt, *Journal of Remedial Education*, **20** (2).

Gulliford, R. (1985) *Teaching Children with Learning Difficulties*. Windsor: NFER-Nelson.

Hanko, G. (1985) *Special Needs in Ordinary Classrooms*. Oxford: Basil Blackwell.

Hinson, M. and Hughes, M. (eds) (1982) *Planning Effective Progress*. Amersham: Hulton/National Association for Remedial Education.

Hodgson, A., Clunies-Ross, L. and Hegarty, S. (1984) *Learning Together:*

Teaching Pupils with Special Educational Needs in the Ordinary School.
Windsor: NFER-Nelson.

Male, J. and Thompson, C. (1985) *The Educational Implications of Disability: A
Guide for Teachers*. RADAR, 25 Mortimer Street, London, W1N 8AB.

McConkey, R. and McCormack, B. (1983) *Breaking Barriers, Educating People
About Disability*. Human Horizons Series, London: Souvenir Press.

McCreesh, J. and Maher, A. (1974) *Remedial Education: Objectives and
Techniques*. London: Ward Lock Educational.

Morgenstern, F. (1981) *Teaching Plans for Handicapped Children*. London:
Methuen.

Sayer, J. and Jones, N. (eds) (1985) *Teacher Training and Special Educational
Needs*. London: Croom Helm.

Shearer, A. (1981) *Disability: Whose Handicap?* Oxford: Basil Blackwell.

Shipman, V. (1979) *Maintaining and Enhancing Early Intervention Gains*.
Princeton, NJ: Educational Testing Service.

Sinson, J. (1985) *Attitudes to Down's Syndrome: An Investigation of Attitudes to
Mental Handicap in Urban and Rural Yorkshire*. Mental Health Foundation,
8 Hallam Street, London W1N 6DH.

Stones, E. (1970) *Readings in Educational Psychology*. London: Methuen.

Swann, W. (ed.) (1981) *The Practice of Special Education*. Oxford: Basil
Blackwell and Open University Press.

Thomas, D. (1978) *The Social Psychology of Childhood Disability*. London:
Methuen.

Thomas, D. (1982) *The Experience of Handicap*. London: Methuen.

Topliss, E. (1982) *Social Responses to Handicap*. London: Longman.

Walkerdine, V. (1984) 'Developmental psychology, the child-centred
pedagogy: the insertion of Piaget into early education.' In J. Henriques,
W. Hollway, C. Urwin, C. Venn and V. Walkerdine, *Changing the Subject*.
London: Methuen.

Warnock, M. (Chairman) (1978) *Special Educational Needs*. London: HMSO.

Wedell, K. (1983) Assessing special educational needs, *Secondary Education
Journal*, **13** (2) June.

Wolfendale, S. (1983) *Parental Participation in Children's Development and
Education*. London: Gordon and Breach Science Publishers.

Wolfendale, S. and Bryans, T. (1979) *Identification of Learning Difficulties: A
Model for Intervention*. Stafford: National Association for Remedial
Education.

Vincent, D. and de la Mare, M. (1985) *New Macmillan Reading Analysis*.
Basingstoke: Macmillan.

Home and school milieux for meeting children's needs

The latter half of the 1980s is an opportune time to look back and chart developments in home–school links since the publication of the Plowden Report and its seemingly simple assertion 'by involving the parents, the children may be helped' (Plowden 1967, para 114). In fact, that assertion was based on the early findings from the American programme Head Start, as well as a heart-felt conviction by the Plowden committee that, as parents are children's 'primary educators', then professionals' support of their direct involvement with their children's development and education could only be beneficial.

What constitutes 'benefit' to children in these terms was closely examined in a review of developments in parental involvement (Wolfendale, 1983). In that book, I set out a rationale to this growing area and put forward recommendations for the development of LEA and school policies on working with parents.

This chapter sets out to draw together a number of recent and current prime initiatives within primary and special education that bear testimony to the effectiveness of such co-operation. They also provide us with clues as to how successfully to instigate and maintain a way of working which had traditionally been alien to the British educational system but which can, and perhaps should, routinely be part of schools' provision. In so doing, there will be an intentional match between principles and practice for this is the pre-eminent area that links education with the community and the wider society.

The 'ideology' of this chapter explicitly embraces the view that it is the responsibility of teachers, schools, and LEAs to ensure that all adults who have care of children and control over them, and responsibilities for their education and welfare work together for their benefit. The belief system propounded in this chapter eschews exhortation, however, and has a bias towards a presentation of current thinking and work that illuminates and substantiates these views.

Parental involvement is a contemporaneous issue that reverberates in national and local political circles. All the main political parties have declared a commitment to increase significantly parental input into decision making, and advocate an extension of consumer choice into educational spheres. 'Parent power', a phrase used in the media and by politicians, however, refers to different faces of the same coin, depending upon party dogma. The enthusiastic espousal of parental rights by politicians of all shades may be less inspired by genuine conviction than by the fact that there has been a demonstrable and impressive groundswell of action and commitment by 'ordinary' people, parents, teachers and other practitioners. Thus it behoves politicians to endorse the electorate in this way. I have participated in various parental involvement initiatives over several years and so the chapter will draw upon some of this work, as it is seen to be central to the spirit of this book.

Children's special educational needs are best appraised within a whole-school context and each child has equal, though uniquely differing, access to curriculum and other opportunities offered by the school. Thus, a school that includes parental involvement as part of its provision potentially offers all children on its roll the chance to benefit. Chapter 1 sought to realign practice in primary education with that of remedial/special education, in order to delineate how special educational needs can be met within primary settings. By the same token, this chapter will, in part, explore how recent, identifiable, good practice in parental involvement in primary schools and special education settings can provide models for primary special needs practice.

En route towards the goal of proposing a viable framework within which parents, teachers, and those from other agencies, can operate, a number of related issues will also be considered. These include the notions of empowerment, partnership, responsibilities towards the propagation of parental involvement, and, finally, the reality of where schools and their teachers, homes and families are located, in contemporary multicultural communities.

THE ATTITUDES OF TEACHERS AND PARENTS

A certain circularity characterises arguments about parental involvement in schools that are based on partial information. That is to say, how do we know if innovative practice comes about as a function of changed attitudes or whether attitudes are changed as a consequence of trying it out? Can teachers and parents be coerced into co-operative ventures by those with the influence to instigate (head teachers, advisers, educational psychologists, for example) when their conviction and enthusiasm are lacking?

The nature of innovation and the persuasive effects these ventures can have may mask, even obliterate, latent resistance. The information we have to hand as to the extent and enthusiasm of parental involvement can only be partial, since we are describing dynamic forces that are already operational, and so the task of keeping a check upon evolving practice becomes well-nigh impossible. It is difficult to keep an accurate and updated chronicle on initiatives that are taking place all over the country, and, sometimes, in schools where teachers and parents may be unaware that their work represents a phenomenon of our times.

Elsewhere, I have been somewhat critical of some survey work into teachers' and parents' attitudes:

> When researchers present teachers with closed hypothetical issues which allow for *existing* perceptions to be expressed, it is not surprising that results which rely on confirmations of the status quo are used to make sterile projections into the future. ... we have moved past the point where we need to sample static opinion towards a point in time when more serious issues relating to policy-into-practice should be aired.
> (Wolfendale, 1983, page 59)

Now, as we move towards the end of the 1980s, we can attest to manifest change in attitude in the existence of many well-maintained parental involvement ventures and smoothly functioning home–school links, whatever the genesis and the original impetus were. Their success buries myths that earlier attitude surveys uncovered concerning parents' perceptions of teachers' inaccessibility and teachers' perceptions of parents' indifference. Views recently expressed have been within contexts of some degree of active and viable parent–teacher co-operation. These are briefly exemplified below, and demonstrate some commonality in views between teachers and parents in mainstream and special education settings. Since views can be held about and expressed on any number of educational issues, only a brief, selective dip will be made into parents' and teachers' views pertinent to the areas with which this book is concerned.

PARENTS' VIEWS

Some studies on parental involvement in reading (Griffiths and Hamilton, 1984, and see Topping and Wolfendale, 1985) have sought parental views as part of evaluation. Notwithstanding a perhaps predictable halo effect, their attitudes to this particular form of parental involvement with the curriculum have been positive and enthusiastic – they feel that their knowledge of the reading process (teaching and learning) has been enhanced, they are clearer about schools' own methods and goals, they endorse the ways in which they are welcomed into school (e.g., the provision of a parents' room).

The Thomas Report (1985, chapter 4) into primary education in the Inner London Education Authority canvassed the views of parents concerning the curriculum and confirmed parents' interest in their children's schooling and endorsement for schools' curriculum aims and objectives. Yet parents felt that they did not always know 'by what standards to judge their own child's achievement; they have difficulty in understanding modern methods' (para. 2.8, page 13). Clearly this information – the reported good will and the need to be given up-to-date, precise information are starting points. Indeed, one LEA has now provided this very database to promote effective communication between home and school. The London Borough of Croydon Education Authority, late in 1985, produced a *Guide for Parents: Primary Education in Croydon*. It includes the following: standards and performance, aims and objectives of primary education, the curriculum areas, and a short, half-page section entitled 'Education for a changing world'.

Parents' views on the effects of a 'proper' system of home–school links can be graphic and illuminating. These following quotations provide a momentary snapshot into schemes that appear to pulse with the enthusiasm that the involvement generates:

> All that I have said actually conveys the active side of Home and School link and really there is much more underlying. I don't believe a welcoming environment could exist if the staff were not welcoming. … 'Links' collective ability to let children be themselves and grow and let the parents be themselves, is remarkable.
> (Parent, Telford Home and School Link Project 1977–1984, page 21)

> The scheme has helped me as much as my child. I have met several people. My child seems confident about going to school.
> (Parent, Milton Keynes Home–School Link Report 1981, page 25)

(Also see accounts from the Liverpool Parent Support programme and Coventry via the selected case studies in Rennie (1985) and the study carried out by Tizard, Mortimore and Burchell (1981).)

Turning now to the views of parents of children with special needs, those who have been or are in receipt of PORTAGE attest unequivocally to its specific benefits *vis-à-vis* the child's acquisition of skills and developmental progress, as well as to the wider advantages (Jordan and Wolfendale in Cameron, 1986). PORTAGE evaluation studies (Bendall, Smith and Kushlick, 1984; Myatt, 1984) include feedback of 'consumer' views. It is therefore likely that the endorsement of the PORTAGE model (its technology, methodology, structure and multidisciplinary and partner emphases) by parents contributed to the present government's explicit backing of POR-TAGE via the Education Support Grant to such under-fives home-based intervention. (See also references in table 2.1, 'Major areas of parental involvement in the 1970s and 1980s: some examples'.)

Other parental feedback from joint work was reported in Pugh (1981), and chapter 7, 'Parents and special educational needs', in Wolfendale (1983) provides extensive references to successful joint intervention work (pages 115–119 and see References List B, pages 127–130).

On the broader front of access to information and support whilst their children are going through assessment procedures, representative parent groups expressed their views to the Warnock Committee (1978, chapter 9) and to the Fish Committee (1985). Both of these major reports on special education contain recommendations for closer working links based in part on parents' views. The Parents' Campaign for Integrated Education in London, one of the organisations that gave evidence to the Fish Committee, includes in its aims the fostering of a dialogue with professionals.

Finally, a reference to a survey (Sandow and Stafford, 1986) the findings of which reflect just how much more there is to do in establishing effective working links despite the encouraging evidence. This is particularly pertinent in the arena still quite new to all involved in special education, namely the processes associated with the 1981 Education Act and especially the nature of the collaboration between parents and professionals. Sandow and Stafford uncovered an apparent mismatch of perceptions between parents and professionals and the worrying fact that so many parents had not received clear explanation of and guidance through the procedures (although they had voiced their needs to the Warnock Committee more or less ten years ago!). Some of these points are picked up later in this chapter.

TEACHERS' VIEWS

A similar picture is painted in this section. That is, where there are already viable and active forms of parental involvement the benefits are so evident and so clearly outweigh the perceived disadvantages as to be reflected in the positive, enthusiastic attitudes of teachers. Again, this can be exemplified in parental involvement in reading (Griffiths and Hamilton, 1984; Topping and Wolfendale, 1985). Likewise, the attitudes of several hundreds of teachers (head teachers, class teachers, advisory and support teachers, other responsible post-holders) sampled via a face-to-face questionnaire that I carried out (Wolfendale, 1985a) over the period 1984–1985 (and which continues still) into parental involvement showed a clear connection between a lively amount of parental involvement in schools and a confident belief in its benefits to all concerned.

Winkley (in Cullingford, 1985) discusses the sources of misperceptions of teachers and parents referred to above and goes on to document the programme of parental involvement in the junior school of which he was head teacher. He captures an evolving situation and changing attitudes in these words:

> schools' relationships with parents develop slowly, artfully, over a period of time, to the point where it virtually becomes a tradition, an unspoken expectation for both teachers and parents to behave in certain ways. … new teachers and the parents of new children tend to accept, absorb and develop the tradition. The key factor is that the participants find the time spent worthwhile and enjoyable.
> (page 83)

In a survey of replies by head teachers to a questionnaire asking about parental involvement in schools, one head teacher remarked that it is the consistency and strength of a school's appeal to parents rather than any single approach that leads to a marked change in their attitudes (COPE, no date).

Within the setting of a school for children with moderate learning difficulties, Marra (1984) sets out some of the requisites for successful parent–teacher interaction and a functioning relationship within the school of which he is head teacher. 'Warts and all' are described in the process and he concludes:

> What has been described … reflects parental involvement in its infancy; the objective of educational involvement and the goal of partnership have yet to be reached. However, what have been described are some of the principles for a possible partnership based on experience.
> (Marra, page 145)

That teachers and parents have a great deal in common is an intrinsic part of the rationale of parental involvement programmes, as is spelled out in Topping and Wolfendale (1985) in chapter 1 and summarised in these words: 'This complementarity of "role" is less a neat formula than it is perceived to constitute a framework for cooperative working' (page 12).

This commonality was explored on a parent teacher inservice course described by Davies and Davies (in Cullingford, 1985), the aim of which was to identify the extent to which these parties agreed and disagreed on certain issues seen as fundamental if the dream of parent–teacher partnership were ever to become a reality. These authors, like Marra, on the basis of this and other experience set out requisites, which, for them, include pre and inservice training in part to avoid enthusiastic but hasty adoption of parental involvement schemes that do not rest on carefully thought-through systems of planning, execution, management and evaluation. As one model for such planning, in the area of parental involvement in reading, Topping and Wolfendale (1985) put forward one schema (chapter 32). For parental involvement in other curriculum and learning areas Topping proposed another model (Topping, 1986).

Another example of the way in which survey findings can be used as a basis for planning took place in South West Hertfordshire (1984). The views of teachers and parents were sampled; 'negative' opinions were explored, and these were found often to be based on lack of explanation, blurred lines of communication, fears and stereotyped expectations of teachers' and parents' 'roles'. The surveyors used their findings to point the way to building upon present activities and providing an even more secure foundation for joint operations.

It is likely, too, that under the formalised banner of co-operative ventures, some of the misperceptions, anxieties, defences cited in Dowling and Osborne (1985) are reduced if not eliminated. For example, conjoint problem identification and problem solving can be facilitated. To some extent, parental involvement can be viewed as a 'preventative' approach in that 'problems' can be 'caught' and dealt with before they exacerbate. Reported joint work in this area is rare – later in this chapter there is an outline of practical strategies to bring this about.

Some time has been spent in the preceding discussion on the important issue of attitudes and what it requires for a situation conducive to the promotion of good working relations to be set up. An attempt has been made to weave into the discussion threads from mainstream and special education settings to demonstrate that the requisites are the same and therefore applicable to integrated settings in which special educational needs are being met. Teachers may be expected to have certain knowledge, skills and sensitivities in relation to acute or enduring problems and handicapping conditions. But, within the framework of collective responsibility outlined in chapter 1, the network of caring and informed personnel to liaise closely with parents becomes more feasible.

DEVELOPMENTS IN PARENTAL INVOLVEMENT: AN OVERVIEW

In the earlier discussion there was some reference to current work in parental involvement. The purpose was to show a juxtaposition in time between the earlier uncharted territory where first steps were tentative and the many active programmes of today. This is such a fast-burgeoning area that no one chapter can do justice to the initiatives. Yet, I shall try in this chapter to present an overview of the field. Another main reason for this is to demonstrate the many rich and varied ways in which integrated educational settings can foster productive and rewarding relationships with the parents of all children; so that 'special needs' children are as integrated as the rest by virtue of their parents' involvement in the routines of their schools.

The reader is referred for main overview texts into parental involvement to: Craft, Rayner and Cohen, 1980; Wolfendale, 1983; Cullingford, 1985; Beattie, 1985. In order to assist the reader to pursue specific areas, table 2.1 provides key references to work in hand.

PARTNERSHIP – THE REALITIES

The amount of current work is indeed impressive, and, to date, testimony from participants is positive. There are signs that some of the work is taking root within schools as part of routine provision. Some schools are even evolving a policy on involving parents that becomes the official imprimatur to ventures that may have started in an *ad hoc*, modest way. That is, some of the realities were tested out prior to formal acceptance at 'policy' level.

Some of the work is multidisciplinary, wherein parents contribute and these ventures are seen as part of a wider network of service provision for meeting special needs which is regarded as cost effective and egalitarian (McConkey, 1986). PORTAGE, in which parents are the educators and therefore play the central role, is seen as coming the nearest to a model of parental partnership, and even then some would argue that the final power of decision making (in terms of resource allocation, personnel deployment) is retained by professionals.

There are writers who cast doubt upon the possibility of 'true' partnership coming about. Potts (1983) sees partnership as token-ism, a kind of window-dressing without parents ever really sharing power. Gliedmann and Roth (1981) are of the view that partnership cannot come about until parents oversee and orchestrate the services that professionals provide for their children. They question the almost 'God-given' self-perception of professionals about the omnipotence of their expertise and aver that

> parents of all races and social classes should be able to pick and choose among different experts, obtain outside opinions when

dissatisfied with the services or advice provided by a professional and constantly evaluate the professional's performance in terms of the overall needs of the growing child.
(Gliedmann and Roth, 1981)

Another writer (Hester, 1977, page 266) makes the observation, and this applies to educational and other services for children, that 'citizen participation in particular citizen power, in program policy and management is important in warding off inequitable treatment'.

The possibility of this sort of central managerial role within education and child-focussed services is also raised by Beattie (1985), who sees the potential of much more direct participation by parents/citizens in power sharing as constituting a challenge to traditional tenets about 'where' power should properly reside and who wields it, including control over the curriculum. This raises questions about the parameters of the governors' role whether they be parents or representing other factions (governors' responsibilities and schools' relationships with their governing bodies in relation to special needs policies and practice are discussed in chapter 5 of this book).

In order to demonstrate that partnership need not remain an ideal, an aspiration, some writers with firsthand experience of working as practitioners at the 'interface' with parents have attempted definitions of knowledge, skills and experience (Mittler and McConachie, 1983) 'complementary expertise' (Cunningham and Davis, 1985) and 'equivalent expertise' (Wolfendale, 1983).

These are the key operational concepts which are embedded within an equal dialogue. I have explored how operational these elements can be as, for example, 'equivalent expertise', 'a reciprocal relationship', leading to 'mutual accountability, mutual gain' (Wolfendale, 1983, chapter 2) in an exercise in which parents make an equal contribution to the assessment processes under the 1981 Education Act (Wolfendale, 1985b). I remain optimistic that equality in these enterprises can, if sought, be obtained. However, I acknowledge the transitional, evolving nature of working towards such aims, as expressed by Davie (1985):

> a rational understanding of the dynamic of partnership and collaboration in these terms would not *guarantee* a closer and more effective relationship in working for children, but it might help to structure situations or shift attitudes in ways which could promote progress.
> (Davie, 1985, page 7)

This echoes remarks made by Marra that were quoted earlier in this discussion. Later in this chapter we shall look at what teachers

Table 2.1 *Major areas of parental involvement in the 1970s and 1980s: some examples*

	Areas of involvement	Key sources
Parents coming in to school	Helping with reading	Stierer 1985, Griffiths & Hamilton 1984, Topping & Wolfendale 1985, Young & Tyre 1983
	As para-professionals in the classroom	Wolfendale 1983, chs. 3 & 4, Rennie 1985, Long 1986
Parents as educators at home	Parental involvement in reading, language, maths learning and 'homework'	As above, also Topping 1986, Wolfendale & Bryans 1986
	Parent–teacher workshops	Wolfendale 1983, ch. 7
	PORTAGE	See below
	Parent education	Pugh & De'Ath 1984
Home–school links	School reports	Goacher & Reid 1983
	Written communication (newsletters) in English and Community Languages	Bastiani 1978
	Moves to open files	NUT policy and some LEAs
	Home–school council	Hargreaves Report
	Parent–tutor groups	Hargreaves Report
	Curriculum plans to parents	Hargreaves Report
	Home visiting	Raven 1980
	LEA parents' handbooks	Croydon

Community education/community	
Parents' rooms in school	Liverpool Parent Support Programme
Parents and others attending classes in school	Coventry, Newham
Multidisciplinary work	Fitzherbert in Cullingford 1985
Local and national parents' associations	ACE, CASE
Parents' support groups	Pugh 1981
LEA Community education	Coventry, Newham
Parent governors	
Parents and special needs	
Parental involvement in referral	Brent LEA
Parental involvement in assessment	Wolfendale 1985b & c, Cunningham & Davis 1985
Parental involvement in behaviour and learning programmes	Carr 1980, Westmacott & Cameron 1981, McConkey 1985, Mittler & McConachie 1983, Newson & Hipgrave 1982, Wolfendale 1983, ch. 7
PORTAGE	Cameron 1982, Dessent 1983, Daly et al. 1985, Copley et al. 1986, Cameron 1986

in primary schools committed to meeting children's special educational needs could do to develop policies that *guarantee* participation by parents. How far and how fast along routes towards partnership teachers and their colleagues wish to travel will depend upon their own circumstances and collective will.

However, before we examine this, it would be appropriate to look briefly at the responsibilities of LEAs in this regard.

THE RESPONSIBILITIES OF LOCAL EDUCATION AUTHORITIES

Most innovative work on parental involvement has been initiated by people working within LEA contexts and employed by LEAs, such as teachers, advisers, educational psychologists. Many school-based projects have 'taken off' as a result of corporate endeavours and many localities have provided inservice training to promote further take-up. The field of parental involvement in reading has been particularly fertile. In these ways LEAs have demonstrated their backing, if not commitment, and have therefore exercised some responsibilities in terms of plant, personnel, materials.

There are signs that an increasing number of LEAs are prepared to take on board and implement policies on parental involvement. The few examples to date of the LEA commitment show variation between them as to how far they are currently prepared to go and in what particular areas they are actively pursuing these ideas.

Table 2.2 is a list of several development areas, matched with selected examples of LEAs.

Another development area, one already touched upon but relevant again at this point, is the training provided by some LEAs for school governors (George, 1984), who of course include parents. Training varies from day courses to the local adoption of the Open University course 'Governing Schools'. I have been involved in one LEA's School Governor training that utilises a mix of these approaches, backed up by other types of support, e.g., tutoring. Pertinent to the theme of this book has been an LEA-instigated day training course during 1986 on special educational needs. Governors were provided with an information pack to help them in regard to their responsibilities for special educational needs (see chapter 5).

Thus we have evidence that a number of LEAs are taking seriously their responsibility for ensuring an informed citizenry who themselves have definite responsibilities for and within schools. Brighouse (in Cullingford, 1985), based in part on his experience in Oxfordshire, sets out a number of practical strategies LEAs could

Table 2.2 *Areas of development in parental involvement in selected LEAs*

	Development area and approximate dates	LEA examples
Parental involvement	Setting up working parties; seconding teachers 1983	Lancashire
	To report back to Ed. Dept., Ed. Committee 1984	Oxfordshire
	Appointment of Adviser for Home–school links, 1985	Oldham
	Home–school liaison from end 1970s	Buckinghamshire
	Educational home visitors since mid 1970s	(Milton Keynes) L. B. Waltham Forest
	PORTAGE	From 1986 via Education Support Grants
Parental involvement in reading	Urban Aid/LEA project into paired reading, since 1984	Kirklees
	PACT since 1980	L. B. Hackney (ILEA)
Community education	Since 1970s	Coventry
	'Going Community' since 1985	L. B. Newham
	Parents' support programme since 1970s	Liverpool
Written information to parents	Primary curriculum booklets 1986	L. B. Brent, L. B. Croydon
	Booklets on primary, secondary and special needs	Many LEAs since 1980

initiate to promote the partnership between schools, homes and the community and, as he says, 'the ideas and possibilities are legion' (page 171).

THE RESPONSIBILITY OF SCHOOLS FOR PARENTAL INVOLVEMENT

Using much of the preceding discussion in this chapter as a frame of reference, and drawing upon the now considerable body of reported work (see chart above), this section aims to set out a model for primary schools to further develop their home–school links within their overall policies on children with special educational needs. The philosophy is very much in tune with the principles sketched out in chapter 1, that is, there can be no separate policy on parental involvement for special needs. However, it is consistent with the insistence that children's special educational needs can and should be met within ordinary schools that due attention should be paid by schools to the development of forms of parental participation that promote, if they do not guarantee, meeting children's needs. Research findings from America and the United Kingdom and other European countries unequivocally point to demonstrable gain by children from any one or more identifiable group (Wolfendale, 1983; Macbeth, 1984; Mittler and McConachie, 1983; Topping, 1986 and McConachie, 1986).

Practical guidelines and planning checklists abound for the introduction, implementation, maintenance and evaluation of parental involvement and home–school links. Here is a list of several (details in references at the end of this chapter):

* *Keeping the School Under Review: The Primary School* (ILEA, 1982)
* Cunningham and Davis 1985
* McConkey 1985
* Topping 1986
* NARE 'Guidelines No. 7' (currently in draft form).

Even though these guidelines tend to be presented in sections, conceptual or taxonomic frameworks are less common. I have attempted (Wolfendale, 1983, chapter 10) to provide one that makes a match between the abstract concepts and their applications in practice. This is reproduced on p. 29 as an exemplar.

IMPLEMENTING A POLICY ON PARENTAL PARTICIPATION

The many elements that go to make a comprehensive parental

PARENTS INTO SCHOOLS

Area	Type	Focus
Concrete and practical	Basic help with learning; fund-raising and support; practical skills; social meetings	Classroom and school
Pedagogical and problem-solving	Syllabus design and planning; co-tutoring of school and home-based learning (general education, remedial, special education needs); school-based discussion of progress	Curriculum
Policy and governing	Educational decision-making; parents as governors	School as institution
Communal	Groups for parents and children (workshops, classes, courses, talks, demonstrations)	School and community

SCHOOL TO HOME

Area	Type	Focus
Information	Verbal, written communication – letters, reports, newsletters, booklets, check and recording systems	Home and parents
Support	Home visiting (enquiry, counselling, relations-fostering); imparting information; discussion of child progress	Home and family
Instruction	Educational home visitor/teaching brief (handicap, special educational needs disadvantage, preschool)	Home, child and parents
Representation	Input by schools into rest of community (resource sharing, resource loan, local meeting place, focal place for cooperative learning)	Home and community

Reproduced from *Parental Participation in Children's Development and Education*. S. Wolfendale, 1983. Tables 3 and 4, page 184.

involvement programme are presented in figure 2.1 in the form of a wheel. The purpose of this form of representation is severalfold; it aims to:

1. Demonstrate the intimate connections between the school, the home, and the community, indeed, the 'reciprocal' nature of the interaction.
2. Make the point to readers that in most schools some form of parental contact and involvement has been well-established over a number of years.

3. Reiterate that this represents a comprehensive programme, possibly goals towards which schools might work.
4. Illustrate how policy, practice and provision on special needs can be incorporated into general parental involvement structures.

The five texts listed below are British sources, each of which describes in various ways many of the ideas set out in the wheel from firsthand experience.

- Tizard, Mortimore and Burchell 1981
- Mittler and McConachie 1983
- McConkey 1985
- Thomas Report 1985, chapter 8
- Long 1986.

Also recommended are the following texts, which are obtainable in the United Kingdom and which are packed with practical suggestions based on theory and research findings:

- Morrison 1978
- Rutherford and Edgar 1979
- Paul 1981
- Berger 1983
- Lombana 1983.

It is proposed that primary school staff, in conjunction with parents and other support staff, formulate a threefold plan of action to involve:

1. reviewing existing parental involvement
2. reviewing current policy and provision on special educational needs (see chapter 7)
3. reformulating parental involvement to incorporate special educational needs.

This may necessitate devising a goal plan and setting out a timetable for achieving short and longer-term goals.

As can be seen, the wheel includes some elements that can routinely be part of parental involvement yet could also be applicable to working with parents of children with acknowledged special educational needs as and when this is appropriate. To effect these working links in practice involves equating 1 + 2 (above) to equal = 3. Thus, from summing 1 + 2, it is possible to abstract these elements from those activities which are denoted on the wheel:

- noting and sharing concerns
- referral
- assessment

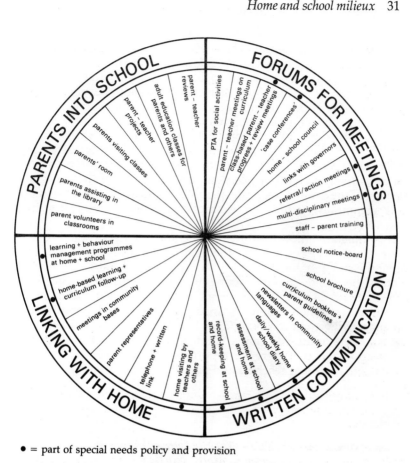

● = part of special needs policy and provision

Figure 2.1 The wheel: a programme of parental involvement

● action and intervention
● recording
● review

Each of these 'special needs' *vis-à-vis* parental involvement will be picked up and pursued in the relevant chapters of this book. The elements are finally seen to cohere once more in chapter 7.

SCHOOL IN THE COMMUNITY

It was announced at the outset of this chapter that there would be an explicit commitment to the involvement of parents in their children's development and education. The rationales for this stance have been more fully discussed elsewhere (Wolfendale, 1983;

McConachie in Coupe and Porter, 1986) and the chapter abounds with references to research and practice in this area.

The ecological perspective has always been central to these rationales (Bronfenbrenner, 1979; Hobbs, 1978) and there are those who, like this author, aver that it is more or less axiomatic that parental involvement is synonymous with an approach that sees school as being centrally part of the child's world, along with home, family, peers, friends, social institutions, and the neighbourhood. Writers like Apter (1982) perceive the 'problems' of children not so much as 'within child' problems as problems within these wider systems. The moves towards parental participation/partnership and community education exemplify ecological principles in practice.

It is imperative now, within a multicultural society (Tomlinson, 1984; Swann Report, 1985) that can no longer lay claim to monotheistic religious practice, to incorporate into schooling cultural perspectives and customs that reflect pluralist practice. A schism between home and school is no longer tenable in our communities where there is more than one neighbourhood language, where shops sell produce from all over the world, where dress reflects cultural diversity. Young children are entitled, as they grow up, to feel that there is a rapprochement between home and school and that their teachers and parents share common goals on their behalf.

REFERENCES

Apter, S. (1982) *Troubled Children, Troubled Systems*. Oxford: Pergamon.

Bastiani, J. (1978) *Written Communication between Home and School*. University of Nottingham, School of Education.

Beattie, N. (1985) *Professional Parents*. Lewes: Falmer Press.

Bendall, S., Smith, J. and Kushlick, A. (1984) *National Study of Portage-type Home Teaching Services: A Research Report, No. 162*. Health Care Evaluation Research Team, University of Southampton, 45/47 Salisbury Road, Highfield, Southampton, Hants.

Berger, E. (1983) *Beyond the Classroom, Parents as Partners in Education*. London: C. V. Mosby.

Bowers, T. (ed.) (1984) *Management and the Special School*. London: Croom Helm.

Bronfenbrenner, U. (1979) *The Ecology of Human Development, Experiments by Nature and Design*. Cambridge MA: Harvard University Press.

Cameron, R. J. (ed.) (1982) *Working Together: Portage in the U.K.* Windsor: NFER-Nelson.

Cameron, R. J. (ed.) (1986) *Portage, Parents and Professionals: Helping Families with Special Needs*. Windsor: NFER-Nelson.

Carr. J. (1980) *Helping your Handicapped Child*. Harmondsworth: Penguin.

COPE (Committee on Primary Education) (no date) *School–Home–Community Relationships*: examples of how some Scottish nursery and primary schools relate to parents and members of the wider community. Moray House College of Education.

Copley, M., Bishop, M. and Porter, J. (eds) (1986) *Portage: More than a Teaching Programme*. Windsor: NFER-Nelson.

Coupe, J. and Porter, J. (eds) (1986) *The Education of Children with Severe Learning Difficulties: Bridging the Gap Between Research and Practice*. London: Croom Helm.

Craft, M., Rayner, J. and Cohen, L. (eds) (1980) *Linking Home and School*, 3rd edn. London: Harper and Row.

Cullingford, C. (ed.) (1985) *Parents, Teachers and Schools*. London: Robert Royce.

Cunningham, C. and Davis, H. (1985) *Working with Parents*. Milton Keynes: Open University Press.

Daly, B., Addington, J., Kerfoot, S. and Sigston, A. (eds) (1985) *Portage: the Importance of Parents*. Windsor: NFER-Nelson.

Davie, R. (1985) *Equalities and Inequalities in Working Together for Children, in Partnership with Parents: a Contrast in Stress*. Partnership Paper No. 6, National Children's Bureau, 8 Wakley Street, London. EC1V 7QE.

Dessent, T. (ed.) (1983) *What is Important about Portage?* Windsor: NFER-Nelson.

Dowling, E. and Osborne, E. (eds) (1985) *The Family and the School, A Joint Systems Approach to Working with Children*. London: Routledge and Kegan Paul.

Fish, J. (Chair) (1985) *Educational Opportunities for All?* The Report of the Committee reviewing provision to meet special educational needs. London: ILEA.

George, A. (1984) *Resource-based Learning for School Governors*. London: Croom Helm.

Gliedman, J. and Roth, W. (1981) 'Parents and professionals' in W. Swann (ed.) *The Practice of Special Education*. London: Basil Blackwell and Open University Press.

Goacher, B. and Reid, M. (1983) *School Reports to Parents*. Windsor: NFER-Nelson.

Griffiths, A. and Hamilton, D. (1984) *Parent, Teacher, Child*. London: Methuen.

Hargreaves, D. (Chairman) (1984) *Improving Secondary Schools*. London: ILEA.

Harris, J. (ed.) (1986) *Child Psychology in Action; Linking Research and Practice*. London: Croom Helm.

Hester, P. (1977) Evaluation and accountability in a parent-implemented early intervention service, *Community Mental Health Journal*, **13** (3) pp. 261–7.

Hobbs, N. (1978) Families, schools and committees: an ecosystem for children, *Teachers' College Record*, **79** (4) May.

ILEA (1982) *Keeping the School Under Review: The Primary School*.

Lombana, J. (1983) *Home–school Partnerships: Guidelines and Strategies for Educators*. New York: Grune and Stratton.

London Borough of Croydon Education Authority (1985) Guide for Parents, *Primary Education in Croydon*.

Long, R. (1986) *Parental Involvement in Primary Schools*. Basingstoke: Macmillan.

Macbeth, A. (1984) *The Child Between: A Report on School–Family Relations in the Countries of the European Community*. Brussels: EEC.

McConachie, H. (1986) *Parents and Mentally Handicapped Children: A Review of Research Issues*. London: Croom Helm.

McConkey, R. (1985) *Working with Parents: A Practical Guide for Teachers and Therapists*. London: Croom Helm.

Marra, M. (1984). 'Parents of children with moderate learning difficulties' in Bowers, T. (ed.) *Management and the Special School*. London: Croom Helm.

Milton Keynes Home–School Link, Report (1981).

Mittler, P. and McConachie, H. (eds) (1983) *Parents, Professionals and Mentally Handicapped People*. London: Croom Helm.

Morrison, G. (1978) *Parent Involvement in the Home, School and Community*. London: Charles E. Merrill.

Myatt, R. (1984) *Report of the Independent Evaluation of the South Lakeland Advisory Service*. University of Exeter.

NARE (forthcoming) Guidelines No. 7: *Guidelines for Involving Parents in Special Projects Concerning the Education of Their Child*. National Association for Remedial Education.

Newson, E. and Hipgrave, T. (1982) *Getting Through to Your Handicapped Child*. Cambridge: Cambridge University Press.

Paul, J. (1981) *Understanding and Working with Parents of Children with Special Needs*. New York: Holt, Rinehart and Winston.

Plowden, B. (Chair) (1967) *Children and their Primary Schools*. London: HMSO.

Potts, P. (1983) 'What difference would integration make to the professionals?' in T. Booth and P. Potts (eds) *Integrating Special Education*. Oxford: Basil Blackwell.

Pugh, G. (1981) *Parents as Partners*. London: National Children's Bureau.

Pugh, G. and De'Ath, E. (1984) *The Needs of Parents*. Basingstoke: Macmillan.

Rennie, J. (ed.) (1985) *British Community Primary Schools*. Lewes: Falmer Press.

Raven, J. (1980) *Parents, Teachers and Children: A Study of an Educational Home Visiting Scheme*. Sevenoaks: Hodder and Stoughton for the Scottish Council for Research in Education.

Rutherford, R. and Edgar, E. (1979) *Teachers and Parents, A Guide to Interaction and Cooperation*. Boston MA: Allyn and Bacon.

Sandow, S. and Stafford, P. (1986) Parental perceptions and the 1981 Education Act. *British Journal of Special Education*, **13** (1) pp. 19–21, March.

Stierer, B. (1985) School reading volunteers: results of a postal survey of primary school head teachers in England. *Journal of Research in Reading*, **3** (1) pp. 21–31.

South West Hertfordshire Teachers' Centre (1984) *Parents and Schools*. Tolpits Lane, Watford.

Swann, Lord M. (Chairman) (1985) *Education for All*. Report of the

Committee of Enquiry into the education of children from ethnic minority groups. London: HMSO.

Telford (Shropshire) *Home and School Link Project* (1977–1984).

Tizard, B., Mortimore, J. and Burchell, B. (1981) *Involving Parents in Nursery and Infant Schools*. London: Grant McIntyre.

Thomas, N. (Chair) (1985) *Improving Primary Schools*. Report of the Committee of Enquiry on Primary Education. London: ILEA.

Tomlinson, S. (1984) *Home and School in Multicultural Britain*. London: Batsford.

Topping, K. (1986) *Parents as Educators*. London: Croom Helm.

Topping, K. and Wolfendale, S. (eds) (1985) *Parental Involvement in Children's Reading*. London: Croom Helm.

Warnock, M. (Chair) (1978) *Special Educational Needs*. London: HMSO.

Westmacott, E. V. S. and Cameron, R. J. (1981) *Behaviour Can Change*. Basingstoke: Macmillan.

Wolfendale, S. (1983) *Parental Participation in Children's Development and Education*. New York and London: Gordon and Breach.

Wolfendale, S. (1985a) 'Questionnaire to teachers on parental involvement: results from a survey', Unpublished documents. Psychology Department, North East London Polytechnic.

Wolfendale, S. (1985b) *Parental contribution to Section 5 (1981 Education Act) Assessment Procedures*. Spastics Society.

Wolfendale, S. (1985c) Involving parents in assessment: exploring parental profiling and the parental contribution to the 1981 Education Act Section 5 Assessment and Statementing Procedures, in *NCSE (National Council for Special Education) Research Exchange*, **4**, September.

Wolfendale, S. and Bryans, T. (1986) *WORD PLAY: Language Activities for Young Children and their Parents*. Stafford: National Association for Remedial Education.

Young, P. and Tyre, P. (1983) *Dyslexia or Illiteracy: Realising the Right to Read*. Milton Keynes: Open University Press.

Planning and managing learning

The territory of special needs was mapped out in chapter 1, and the complexities of the concept were examined. It was readily acknowledged that teachers have a juggling act to perform; they are encouraged to recognise the special needs of all children in their charge, and urged at the same time to be alert and sensitive to individual needs.

It is possible that the notion of learning difficulties and deficit models arose in part from teachers' need to manage their classrooms and that to posit a separate 'breed' of children with learning and behaviour difficulties helped them to organise the mainstream of the classroom, and enabled them, with justification, to call upon remedial teachers to help with the harder-to-teach children.

At the heart of this book lies the philosophy that *all* children have individual needs in learning and other ways, but that the teaching force in any one school can, corporately, manage classrooms and school provision to meet those individual needs. The rhetoric goes beyond calling for attitude-change to the reality of setting out teaching and management objectives to facilitate the planning of learning climates within schools.

SCHOOL AS A CENTRE FOR LEARNING

Children's, and indeed adults', learning takes place anywhere, everywhere, at any time. School-based learning, as it has evolved, is characterised by direction, intention, the provision of tools to assist learning, and the concentration in one setting of adult expertise to facilitate, by formalised means, knowledge and skill acquisition.

Our thinking has evolved over the time-span of this century, from a view of school as a place which promoted rote learning, via drill, to a view which encompasses a plurality of methods and richness of curriculum, set within far broader perspectives. For instance, the aims of education as discussed by Hirst and Peters (1970) would simply not have been thought about, let alone acted upon, at the turn of the century when class chanting of reading primers was common and children who did not keep up the pace fell by the wayside. Economic factors had primacy over consideration of the education of the whole child.

Contemporary teachers have the central aspiration of aiming to reach and teach each child in their classes, assisting each one to attain his or her potential. However, up to the present, there has not been an obligation upon schools to demonstrate their approaches *vis-à-vis* individual children, and the accountability system, whereby schools have to explain and justify progress and lack of progress, has hardly begun.

I agree with Ainscow and Tweddle (1979) in averring that schools, henceforth, should be accountable to their clientele (children, parents) and to their governing bodies (education, the community). Facilitation of this demanding process can be effected by adoption of the notion of collective responsibility outlined in chapter 1.

These prefatory remarks are intended as the backcloth to this chapter, which adopts a problem-solving approach to learning; that is, children's rate and pace of learning can be observed (process) and what they have 'learned' (e.g., facts, reasoning competence, specific skills) can be measured (product). Learning, for all of us, takes place by means of a mix of approaches or strategies, e.g., trial, error, self-correction, rehearsal, repetition of acts, rote learning, and so on. Our strategies can be viewed as composites of problem-solving devices to assist the learning process, to overcome learning hurdles ('getting stuck', plateauing, needing more opportunity and exposure, practice, etc.).

'Learning difficulties' therefore can be conceptualised as something all adults can experience at any point in acquiring facts or new skills (changing the wheel of a car, mending a watch, memorising the itinerary of a touring holiday). This analogy with adult learning is a deliberate reminder that learning is a continuous and continuing process and we start to employ our problem-solving strategies very early on as young children.

The pedagogic responsibilities of teachers and others in education is to enable and assist children to:

- understand the point and purpose of the learning tasks presented to them and in which they engage
- learn how to learn
- evolve effective learning strategies
- identify learning hurdles, 'sticking-points' along the way and apply appropriate problem-solving learning strategies.

The direct and conscious involvement of all children in their own learning has not been a feature of primary schools. So many children who experience some learning blockage have not traditionally been enabled to identify the source of their difficulty at an early enough point in time to want to take action, to co-operate with others acting on their behalf. With reference to the literature, I (Wolfendale, 1980) listed a number of early precursors to later learning failure, and expressed the view that if these could be identified and acted upon much earlier, a significant number of potential later referrals could be avoided. Indeed, the whole screening 'movement' (Bullock, 1975; Wolfendale and Bryans, 1979) was reliant on the view, itself based on plenty of 'case' and survey evidence, that early identification of early-appearing learning difficulties linked to intervention was a justifiable preventive approach.

Indeed, since the exploratory earlier days of screening, in the mid 1970s, methods of identification linked with setting curriculum objectives and good planning have become more sharply focussed and closely targeted and methods of evaluation are more refined. Some of these approaches will be discussed later in the chapter.

With Trevor Bryans (Wolfendale and Bryans, 1980) I explored some of these 'prereferral' aspects of learning difficulty. We identified them as being subtle, not always noticeable, but accruing signs of temporal difficulties with learning material (e.g., beyond the child's present skill level, too demanding in amount, unclear in presentation and explanation by teacher, totally missing due to child absence from school during a key lesson, etc.). Concomitant with these difficulties were early, again subtle, signs of learning-associated stress, lowered morale ('can't cope') and reduced motivation ('won't try to'). The small-scale intervention project we carried out enabled us to observe and record, first-hand, the performance and responses of a small group of six- to seven-year-old children who had been identified by their teachers (using the Croydon Checklist as an early school progress guide) as showing early-appearing learning difficulties. We felt that irrespective of 'ability', which we decided was not relevant to assess, the children in question could be enabled to overcome their embryonic difficulties and be assisted to develop appropriate learning strategies and maintain learning motivation.

SCOPE OF THE CHAPTER

From this introductory discussion, the aim is now to look at changing practice in assessing children's learning, and planning and executing learning programmes. This standpoint of current and evolving practice will then lead into a rather more prospective examination as to how effectively to create conditions for learning.

The chapter is about the right of all children to be in receipt of learning experiences that will enable them to reach their potential.

In the words of Fish (1985) such a view 'stretches the concepts of learning and teaching far beyond the basic skills of literacy and numeracy ... it redefines education as any systematic intervention provided to enhance personal growth and development.' (Fish, 1985, page 12).

Whether or not some children are 'slow learners', have sensory or physical handicaps that preclude the adoption of some of the more usual methods of information and skill acquisition, the starting point of curriculum planning is each child's 'teachable self' (Hanko, see end of chapter 1), and the formulation of a learning profile that identifies learning assets and locates learning strategies. The chapter, in toto then, aims to represent a mix of practice within theoretical and conceptual frameworks, and, as such, aims to herald the more specific areas that are the subjects of the other books in this primary series.

The message contained in the medium of this introductory book, and particularly in this chapter is thus that: irrespective of degree and complexity of special need and irrespective of the extent and type of integration adopted by any one school, the principles outlined in this chapter are applicable to all children (Evans, 1985). From the principles can be derived a learning formula applicable uniquely to each child, a theorem that has to be proved in practice.

CHANGE AND TRANSITION

A government report on education can be regarded as a marker for future practice in that it presents a comprehensive picture of what the report defines as existing good practice, and, so doing, validates that practice.

So it is with the Warnock Report, which is credited with being pace-setting and a beacon for special education practice (Welton, Wedell and Vorhaus, 1982). Certainly, the models of integration, inter-agency co-operation, and parental involvement considered by Warnock are, with justification, used as markers. Some of the practice the Committee referred to was already manifest but not then widespread. Specifically, in terms of learning and, more particularly, learning difficulties, this related to moves away from IQ testing and towards early identification, curriculum-based assessment, and broadening the role and function of remedial teachers to encompass a special needs brief.

The metamorphosis of remedial teachers from an amateurish, low-status adjunct within schools (this author has been, at various stages, a remedial teacher) into a better organised corps of professionals with clearer, wider terms of reference is one of the phenomena within changing special education.

These developments, up to the present, have been chronicled (Gains and McNicholas, 1979; Brennan, 1982; Gulliford, 1985; Smith, 1985) and are still in flux. For instance, the recommendation in Warnock to abolish the distinction between remedial and special education has been translated in so many LEAs into the appointment of an adviser for special needs, with the all encompassing brief to unite what passed for remedial and special educational provision under one banner. Likewise, an increasing number of LEAs are strengthening the links between special and mainstream schools, where they may have no explicit policy on integration, and exploring how remedial/special teachers can most effectively work with mainstream staff. Those LEAs with an avowed programme of working towards integrated provision incorporate into their blueprints a definite and key place for their cohorts of ex-remedial now turned 'special needs teaching and advisory personnel' (see Gipps and Gross, 1984, for a list of contemporary names for support services).

Attention will now turn to several key aspects of planning learning and responding to children's learning hurdles that are the proper province within primary schools of a combination of class and advisory teachers in co-operation with other staff, parents, and support services (see chapter 5). First, however, some reference will be made to the concept of learning difficulties, as this has been so influential in guiding the development of services and directing the deployment of personnel.

LEARNING DIFFICULTIES: A REAPPRAISAL

There is an inevitable focus on 'learning difficulties' in the bulk of this chapter, with the broader, more positive perspectives on learning considered towards the end. I consider that the emphasis on difficulties to the exclusion of contexts of and conditions for learning has contributed to the separatist traditions already noted and the divisions made between children with learning problems and those without.

Concepts of learning difficulties continue to vex all of us in education. It was noted (Wolfendale, 1980) that in the United Kingdom the term 'specific learning difficulties' was not uniformly acceptable (and especially with its connotation if not synonymity with dyslexia, cf. Farnham-Diggory, 1978) and in fact regarded with ambivalence (Tansley and Pankhurst, 1981).

The official definition of learning difficulties in the Education Act 1981 with its reference to norm yardsticks does little to clarify how the concept could be put into operation (Wedell, 1983). Gulliford (1985) provides a chapter that aims to clarify and explore the types and relativities of learning difficulties. Earlier, I sought to elicit first-hand definitions by teachers themselves of the term, and received responses from 60 teachers of all age-groups. These responses confirmed that there is a wide variety in viewpoint, description and explanation, ranging from:

- *performance deficit* 'inability to concentrate for any length of time, poor memory, lack of co-ordination' (junior class teacher); 'slowness in acquiring knowledge' (infant school maths responsibility)
- *mix of deficit and home circumstances* 'inability to listen and concentrate for any length of time, combined with a lack of parental interest in what the child does in school' (junior class teacher); 'poor motivation because of emotional or behavioural problems or deprived home circumstance' (secondary teacher);

Some mentioned 'lack of ability', which Stott (1978) has criticised for the equation of intelligence with learning ability. Very few referred to teaching or school-based factors. So, from practitioners to researchers and theorists, it does seem that there is no standard or generally accepted concept of learning difficulties, but rather a use of the term that is essentially pragmatic: 'a response to perceived needs and an expedient means for allocating resources on a locally agreed priority basis' (Wolfendale, 1980, page 115). The term then provides blanket coverage for underachievement and for 'slow' learners (cf. Gulliford, 1985, chapter 3 for categories of mild, moderate, severe, and specific learning difficulties).

This book extends its use to include the lack of any match between a child's learning needs and teaching/learning opportunities to meet these needs. The needs may become 'special' if a disability in one or more areas handicaps a child's efficient learning and she or he has to be enabled to utilise other media, for example:

- a visual disability could call for use of auditory and tactile means (use of other senses)
- a hearing impairment could call for the use of non-verbal communication, signing systems
- a physical disability could call for the use of technological or other aids, like computers.

The reader is referred to recent texts on integration which explore these matches in more depth (Hodgson, Clunies-Ross and Hegarty, 1984).

RESPONDING TO LEARNING DIFFICULTIES: WITH REFERENCE TO BEHAVIOURAL FRAMEWORKS

There are well-documented accounts of attitudes and provision in the United Kingdom from the 1950s on learning difficulties in mainstream schools that have concentrated in the main on slow progress with the basic subjects (Tansley and Gulliford, 1960; McCreesh and Maher, 1974). Considerable expertise in these mainly remedial approaches was built up and paved the way for the 'newer' approaches of the early 1970s in identifying and assessing children's early-appearing learning difficulties (Wolfendale and Bryans, 1979). In turn, the requisites identified by these and other authors (Stott 1978; Leach and Raybould, 1977) led to contemporary developments, characterised as 'teaching by objectives', and 'curriculum-based assessment', which, in general, are grounded in theories of behavioural psychology and represent the application in educational settings of these theoretical frameworks. The work of Ainscow, Tweddle and their colleagues, which was first described in their seminal book *Preventing Classroom Failure: An Objectives Approach* (Ainscow and Tweddle, 1979), has generated widespread application of their ideas and a considerable number of further developments. Their work, targeted mainly to children with learning difficulties in mainstream or schools for children with moderate learning difficulties, has been paralleled by similarly behaviourally based approaches for children with severe learning difficulties, e.g., PORTAGE (Bishop, Copley and Porter, 1986, is the most recent book; see NFER-Nelson catalogue for the others in the PORTAGE series) and the Education of the Developmentally Young (EDY–McBrien, 1981).

The basic tenets of these approaches are that they:

- obviate any need for psychometrics assessment when an inherent, prime purpose is to probe and pin-point precisely a child's task performance in relation to the curriculum areas on which he or she is currently working
- provide opportunities for teachers who know a child best to record his or her current mastery as a basis for planning the next stages
- promote, via their techniques, the idea of positive intervention with a child's learning rather than the deficit model with its undue emphasis on a child's failure
- encourage the notion that the assessment through teaching model is applicable to the broader curriculum than just with the basic subjects (see below).

The publication edited by Wheldall (1981) comprised one of the first compendia of current British work and Jewell and Feiler (1985) provide a useful and succinct review of these approaches and describe their growing adoption.

Ainscow and Tweddle went on to produce a second book (1984) that represents an extension of the work described in their first book and that was developed over a period of several years of classroom trials. The materials consist of 122 carefully selected and precisely stated teaching objectives in arithmetic, handwriting, independence (or self-help) skills, language, motor skills, reading, and spelling. In effect the book comprises a nursery, infant, and beginning junior curriculum.

Direct Instruction is another curriculum/method approach (SRA, 1985). Solity (1984) outlines the behavioural principles from which the teaching practice is derived. Whilst DI is associated with being a successful programme within the American Head Start and Follow-through initiatives (Becker et al., 1981), it is intended for all learners and its curricula include reading, arithmetic and mathematics, language, and spelling from ages 6–15 years. In the realms of moderate and severe learning difficulties, Raymond (1984) offers programmes based on teaching by objectives and covering communication, self-help, independence skills, and cognitive tasks, as does Kiernan (1981).

A way of measuring learning that is part of the behavioural 'technology' and that complements the methods and content of learning programmes is precision teaching (Matthews and Booth, 1982; Jewell and Feiler, 1985). Precision teaching is not a method of teaching, but rather a way of trying to find out 'what teaches best' by providing daily feedback on the effectiveness of instruction, and by providing techniques for direct and daily measurement, charting, and evaluation of individual pupils' progress towards mastering of specific educational tasks (Raybould and Solity, 1985).

Jewell et al. describe a system called PETSL (Precise Educational Techniques for Slow Learners) that combines the major features of a number of approaches that can be introduced via an inservice training course for professionals involved in planning structured learning programmes for children experiencing difficulties in acquiring basic academic skills. Teachers or educational psychologists frequently need a clearly defined system for exploring some of the key factors in a child's ability to learn. These factors are fourfold:

1. The task being taught;
2. The teaching method;
3. The materials used, and
4. The child's motivation to learn the task.

These factors can be systematically varied and their influence on the child's learning subsequently recorded and evaluated.

PETSL explores these factors in detail and provides the course participants with skills in writing individual education programmes. The units evolved cover:

- writing objectives
- task analysis
- identifying pupil objectives through placement tests

- individual education programme design
- precision teaching
- direct instruction

The inservice format adopted is similar to that employed by the Education for the Developmentally Young Project (EDY). In this, video, role-play, and practice with children are frequently employed.

The PETSL course is most appropriate for peripatetic teachers in special educational needs, outreach teachers, teachers in special schools, and educational psychologists.

The cornerstone in PETSL and other approaches is the individual education programme. DATAPAC (Daily Teaching and Assessment for Primary Age Children) (Ackerman et al., 1983) is regarded as an assessment through teaching approach for individual children. This 'package' contains assessment materials (use of 'placement' tests), teaching sheets and teaching instructions covering mathematics, reading, handwriting, and spelling.

It has been found to be cost-effective to direct inservice training on these behavioural approaches to groups of teachers within a school, or at a centre, using a dissemination model. An earlier example of the target teacher dissemination model is that of the LEA-backed Croydon Screening Procedures (Wolfendale and Bryans, 1979). Other LEAs have followed suit in adopting a global LEA-backed initiative that aims, in the first instance, simultaneously to reach a number of teachers. A well-known example, and one that has inspired derivatives, is the Coventry SNAP (Special Needs Action Programme) (Ainscow and Muncey, 1983 and 1984). This combines the production of written materials with inservice back-up and support. Other examples of training packages and programmes based on behavioural frameworks come from Birmingham, Cleveland, Leeds, Northamptonshire, and Surrey. The advent of the 1981 Education Act has been a spur to collective action. The theme of INSET is once more picked up in chapter 6.

CURRICULUM APPLICATION OF BEHAVIOURAL FRAMEWORKS

Older-style remediation concentrated in the main on reading and literacy skills, and to a much lesser extent on other major curriculum areas. Behavioural programmes have the flexibility to be subject-focussed where appropriate (e.g. DATAPAC spelling, DISTAR language or maths) and also broader-based (multiple-subject or related skill areas, e.g. self-help skills, as included within

PORTAGE, also see Raymond, 1984). Furthermore, conventional remedial approaches relied on pre and post assessment of children's attainment as measures of progress. But the hallmark of the programmes described above is that assessment is intrinsically part of teaching and is therefore continuous measurement being inbuilt and not grafted onto either end of teaching learning sequences (Tweddle and Pearson, 1984).

There is an intentional interplay between an individual education programme and broader-based curriculum planning and curriculum management, in terms of an objectives approach. Cameron (1981) and Lister and Cameron (1986) present the rationale for applying objectives to curriculum planning and drew attention to the requirements of the 1981 Education Act for children assessed under the Act to have 'the protection of a statement' (see chapter 5). A 'good' statement is one that sets out a child's special (learning and other) needs in detail on the basis of comprehensive educational, psychological, medical, and other assessment, and then goes on to specify exactly how these needs can and should be met.

Lister and Cameron relate this to schools' contexts in these words: 'objectives for children with special needs should therefore be formulated with reference to the school's overall goals' (page 7). They then go on to give a quotation from White and Haring (1980) which sums up the child–curriculum equation:

> We cannot begin to individualise an educational program for a child in a vacuum – we need a larger perspective than any single child ... these expectations take the form of a basic curriculum which translates the school's 'mission' into more specific goals and even more specific objectives which the children are to master at each level in their progress through the school.

Within this model, there is the leeway to progress from very broad teacher management objectives and then onto the specification of a task and attribute analysis.

The sheer specificity of learning programmes, grounded in behavioural principles, set within broader, longer-term curriculum goals, is consistent with the theme of this chapter, that is, the dictates of the curriculum are secondary to the pivotal claims of each child's learning requirements.

CRITIQUES OF BEHAVIOURAL APPROACHES

Lister and Cameron themselves pay some attention to criticisms and possible pitfalls of a curriculum by objectives approach. Critics, peering into behavioural domains have been deadlier in their indictments. For example, Strivens (1981) views behaviour modification (which is related, indeed is a progenitor, to some approaches currently in use and described above) as socially controlling and limiting upon personal autonomy. Thomas (1985) criticises behavioural approaches as not being sufficiently 'context sensitive', whilst Swann (1985) points to the lack of relevance to children's experience outside school of the content of Direct Instruction and DI derived programmes.

To the charges that behaviour modification and teaching by objectives are but benign forms of social control and put restraints on access to other richer sources of experience, a commentary on the applicability of behaviour approaches within the context of this book seems necessary.

Specifying curriculum goals and learning targets is quite consistent with an ecological approach. Paired reading (Topping and Wolfendale, 1985) and PORTAGE exemplify how a specific technique with its own 'rules' can be applied within and out of school contexts). Children's progress is manifest, generalisable, and rewarding to child, teachers, parents, family; 'control' of the curriculum can be demonstrably shared in school and with family/community settings; skills can be shared and pooled (as the principles are not arcane and mysterious, the psychology within them can be readily given away); far from legitimating social control processes (an oft-repeated critics' cry), the curriculum and educational processes are opened up and the content and teaching methods made accountable to all.

Finally, we cannot foretell future educational developments and curriculum technologies; they may or may not evolve from behaviourist teaching approaches. On the basis of 'what to do tomorrow?' (Potts, 1983) we can only try to demonstrate success along provable lines with the techniques we have evolved to date. On pragmatic grounds alone, we are justified at present in using and refining these techniques in each child's interests. The moral imperatives that so concern the critics apply in reverse too.

TOWARDS COLLECTIVE RESPONSIBILITY FOR PLANNING AND MANAGING LEARNING IN PRIMARY SCHOOLS

The previous section sought to demonstrate how behavioural frameworks have increasingly been adopted in schools – in special schools, where objectives-based curricula are now common, as well as in collaborative programmes developed by teachers and educational psychologists in special and mainstream settings. Successful learning programmes (successful by whatever criteria initially agreed by the users) are more likely if certain requisites are inbuilt and adhered to: agreement, sometimes contractual, regularity of application, consistency, clarity of recording and means of evaluation. Rigour is demanded on the part of all participants to guarantee smooth running (and it is undeniable that behavioural approaches are time and labour intensive and committing).

Overall behaviourist assessment and teaching are cost-effective, and, as PORTAGE has demonstrated, an efficient means of service delivery (Wolfendale in Harris, 1986). Thus, one component is teamwork, and behavioural approaches go a fair way to providing a basis for assessment and intervention with learning difficulties. The discussion in this chapter now broadens to encompass other aspects of planning and managing learning in primary schools, of which learning difficulties are a part.

The nub of school-based action is the relative contribution and input of several identified key people in relation to one or more children.

The course of action outlined below is put forward as a possible model, presented sequentially. It is a demonstration of how teamwork and collective responsibility could operate over planning, learning and responding to identifiable learning difficulties and as such links in with the theme of later chapters that deal with co-operation with others, organisation and evaluating classroom practice.

THE LEARNING PROFILE

The idea and definition of a learning profile was introduced in chapter 1 and referred to earlier in this chapter. The formulation rests on the assumption that it is the learning assets of a child as well as learning hurdles that are to be assessed by key personnel and that the outcomes will be used to agree on longer-term goals and shorter-term targets right across the curriculum. The learning profile is the first core part of an individual education programme and stands as a reference point for appraisal and review.

The potential of a learning profile was first tentatively explored during 1979 and 1980 (Wolfendale and Bryans, 1980). We constructed learning profiles on each of six children at the end of a 72-session-long (spanning two terms) language-based/small-group intervention programme. We conceptualised the profiles into four parts that, as a whole, we thought could be used as a basis for forward planning. The four sections are:

1. Specific difficulties with learning.
2. Positive features of learning.

3. Learning needs.
4. Trends (documented during and summarised at the end of the intervention programme).

Examples of completed profiles are given in Wolfendale and Bryans (1980). Later (1982–1983), several MSc educational psychology students at North East London Polytechnic (trainee educational psychologists) compiled learning profiles of children with whom they were working on placement. One, of Kenny, is reproduced in appendix 1. The trainee (Lee Tily) first completed it in November 1982 and later, in the following year, recorded what learning trends and outcomes from intervention were evident. Although at an embryonic stage of development, Kenny's learning profile (entitled 'Profile Analysis' in appendix 1) shows the potential of its use at initial assessment-recording stage as well as its continuing use, at monitoring and review stages. Appendix 1 also contains a copy of notes 'accompanying the use of profile analysis'; these provide the conceptual background and rationale, give guidelines as to its use and contain extracts from two child profiles drawn up from the intervention project (Wolfendale and Bryans, 1980). As can be seen, the learning profile is intended to be applicable to any intervention, teaching by objectives, or other programme approach.

CONTRIBUTING TO A LEARNING PROFILE: TAKING COLLECTIVE ACTION

In illustrating a collective approach, the key personnel referred to above will, for the purposes of this chapter, be seen to be class teacher, advisory/support/special needs co-ordinator, parent, possibly attached educational psychologist, and, where possible, children themselves. Naturally for some children, other people will be involved and will be identifiably part of the network of provision and support. Examples of this will be given later.

Key tasks will be identified, agreed and shared. The learning profile will be initially drawn up based on the contribution of key people; for example, the profile of Kenny shows how parents' views were incorporated.

The various components that contribute to the learning profile (which is a continuous means of recording, analysing, planning) are presented sequentially in Table 3.1, in chart form where appropriate, giving examples of possible inputs. A key reference list is provided for readers who wish to follow up and implement these various strategies. All the references in these sections have a practical basis (contain plenty of suggestions for assessment and

Table 3.1 *Assessment: options for key people*

References Key	Class teacher	Support/advisory teacher	Educational psychologist	Parents	Child
1, 2, 3, 4	Attainment tests (e.g. reading, maths, language)	↕	↕		
5, 6	Criterion-referenced, curriculum-based assessments; placement tests	↕	↕		
7, 8, 9, 10, 11, 12, 13, 14, 15	Performance checklist; profiling; observation	↕	↕	'Child at Home' profile	Self-report
	Attitude inventories	↕	IQ and ability testing		

References key:
1. Pumfrey (1985) **2.** Vincent (1985) **3.** Bentley and Malvern (1983) **4.** Croll and Moses (1985) **5.** Ainscow and Tweddle (1979, 1984) **6.** Akerman et al. (1983) – DATAPAC **7.** Pearson and Lindsay (1986) **8.** 'Child in School Profile' (Primary age) compiled by Bryans and Wolfendale **9.** 'Parental profiling', Wolfendale (1986), also see appendix 2 for Notes for Parents (writing a parental profile; reporting on 'My Child at Home') **10.** Westmacott and Cameron (1981) **11.** Newson and Hipgrave (1982) **12.** ILEA pilot junior age self-report 'Me at School' (rating scale) **13.** Self-reporting: two sample self-report schedules are included in appendix 3. They are representative of various 'home-grown' versions that have been in use in a number of LEAs and can be completed by a child with or without assistance. They can also be adapted. **14.** Leach and Raybould (1977) **15.** Wolfendale and Bryans (1979) for suggestions on observation, also use of the Learning Descriptive Observation Sheet. **16.** Ollendick and Hersen (1984).

Table 3.2 *Intervention: options for key people*

References key

1, 2, 3, 4, 5	*Devise individual programmes,* examples: Direct Instruction; precision teaching DATAPAC; PETSL; parental involvement in reading Peer tutoring	*Classroom organisation* Room management (chapter 5) Seating arrangements Groupwork Timetable
6, 7, 8, 9 10	Children's self-monitoring & recording	

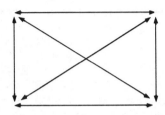

Work with other teachers Peripatetic/visiting advisory teacher School-based advisory/special needs co-ordinator	*Work with support agencies* Educational psychologists Advisors Remedial and resource teachers Community languages Parents

References key:
1. SRA (1985) **2.** Raybould and Solity (1985) **3.** Akerman et al. (1983) **4.** Jewell et al. **5.** Topping and Wolfendale (1985) **6.** Indoe (1986) **7.** Sprick (1981) – this is a comprehensive handbook covering nine topic areas in planning for learning and behaviour management **8.** Lovitt (1984) **9.** Wood (1984) **10.** Willey (1985).

intervention for all learners, irrespective of 'special' needs) or have practical implication for classroom activity. They are asterisked in the reference list at the end of this chapter for readers who wish to follow them up for designing and carrying out practical work.

Other components of a learning profile, such as record-keeping and means of evaluation, are explored further in chapters 5 and 7 respectively, in part because the subject matter of this chapter and that of chapter 4 lend themselves to some common specifications for record-keeping and evaluation.

WITHIN THE CONTEXT OF THE CURRICULUM

The planning and management of the curriculum rightly belongs primarily to curriculum and subject specialists. Where 'collective action' comes in is at points when teachers want to plan appropriate learning opportunities for individual children. The quotation from White and Haring (see earlier, page 45) illuminates how each child's learning needs can be identified and planned for. As she or he moves through curriculum stages (e.g. via objectives for an exact degree of specificity) progress as well as 'sticking points' are likewise identified. The formula, child/curriculum match is applicable to the whole curriculum and not just in traditional approaches to 'failing' children, to the 'key' subjects of reading, mathematics. It is becoming more commonplace nowadays to come across arrangements that are an integral part of classroom practice where special needs/learning resource teachers are helping class teacher colleagues to plan and manage learning in general, and in particular, on behalf of children with special educational needs.

At the risk of labouring the theme, the point is that, whereas, once, opting out of mainstream curriculum into tangential remedial activities appeared to be a viable solution, a view prevails that those 'failing' children's interests are not best served by distancing them from the mainstream. The same applies to children who have been/are in special school who are entitled to access to a broader spectrum of curriculum opportunity. Their protection, within the hurly-burly of an 'ordinary' school comes from a carefully prepared 'statement of needs' – in this chapter's context a learning profile.

Within a framework of agreed and shared responsibility, there is a receptive climate to express and list at an early stage concerns felt about a child and not to wait until the problem becomes 'referrable'. 'Need' is relative; therefore, with the handicapping labels officially dropped, there is all the more reason to abolish the absolutes. The term 'remedial' should henceforth be eliminated from the educational lexicon.

The model (ideal or reality?) is one in which teachers plan the learning environment and 'manage' it on behalf of the learners who proceed through the series of planned learning tasks (in whatever subject area). They are assisted in problem-solving and responding with strategies appropriate to their individual pace and preferred/evolved learning style. And in an age of 'hi-tech', many a child handicapped by disability can be enabled, through the use of electronic equipment, to benefit from the curriculum.

Only if schools can move towards the notion of collective responsibility and corporate management to embrace 'special needs' can we avoid falling into the trap where the old-style remedial department becomes the new-titled special needs department, but separatist practice endures (Galloway, 1985) – a change of name will merely mean the same thing!

POSITIVELY PROMOTING LEARNING

An earlier analysis of the development of learning competence (Wolfendale and Bryans, 1979, chapter 6) referred to writers who predicted that skills will acquire greater importance at the expense of specific pieces of information. More recently Oliver (1982) expressed these views:

> Young people are ready to do far more than we give them credit for and by diagnosing what they can do rather than what they cannot and teaching from this area of competence we can give them the confidence to make, not merely receive, knowledge structures.
> (page 131)

The active promotion of these aspirations into practice is persuasively put forward by Bloom (1983a & b) whose formulation of 'alternative variables' challenges long-held received wisdom about what is and what is not the rightful province of teachers, and what is sacrosanct and therefore unalterable. His five 'alterable variables' are briefly described below. His basic premise is that, as a result of recent educational research, we have a better understanding of teaching–learning factors. As a result, he feels, pupil learning can now be improved greatly, and it is possible to describe the favourable learning conditions that can enable virtually all pupils 'to learn to a high standard'.

BLOOM'S 'ALTERABLE VARIABLES'

1. *Available time versus time-on-task*. Bloom says that we ought to pay more attention to time spent as 'active learning time' rather than on considerations of what time is made available for learning, for not all pupils are equally 'on-task' at any one time. Studies show that the percentage of engaged (on-task) time is highly related to subsequent measures of achievement and to subsequent indices of interests and attitudes towards learning.

2. *Intelligence versus cognitive entry*. Bloom expresses the view that cognitive entry characteristics are more relevant to present and future learning than IQ measures as predictors of learning ability. These are the specific knowledge, abilities and skills that are the

essential prerequisites for learning a particular subject or task. They have a high relation with achievement and have an obvious causal effect on later achievement.

3. *Summative versus formative testing.* As with Gagné (1985), Bloom's work has been concerned with requisites and conditions for children achieving mastery at every level and stage; thorough mastery is an essential precursor for subsequent stages. Yet we have failed to develop and apply checking (formative) tests and procedures to verify each child's mastery level. Our summative tests (end of a course, end of term/year, examinations) are blunt, insensitive measures of progress as well as of task difficulty.

4. *Teachers versus teaching.* Bloom is critical of teachers' traditional practice, which is characterised by a method of proceeding that does not bring out the best in children, as some teachers unwittingly pay more attention to and therefore reward the faster learner.

5. *Parent status versus home environment processes.* In this 'alterable variable', Bloom juxtaposes specific curricular focus on mastery learning with broader, ecological considerations as to what parents and other adults significant in children's lives can contribute. On the basis of evidence, he says that it is clear that when home and school have 'congruent learning emphases' and shared aspirations (see chapter 2, this book) the child has little difficulty in later school learning.

Bloom's optimistic views as to how schools might be enabled to alter expectations, attitudes, organisation, and conditions for learning have been given prominence here because they are compatible with the themes and philosophies of this book in its entirety and with this chapter on learning in particular.

It is not for want of trying that we have not found 'the holy grail' – the formulae by which children's (and adults') potential can be optimised. There is an honourable tradition of American psychologists who have worked for years hypothesis-testing into conditions for learning, e.g. Ausubel (1978), Gagné (1985), Bloom himself, others mentioned earlier and associated with the genesis of behavioural approaches.

Researchers and researcher-practitioners in America and the United Kingdom have focussed on specific strategies to promote efficient learning, e.g. memory (Kail, 1984), learning style (Stott, 1978), and learning strategies (Nisbet and Shucksmith, 1986), learning how to learn (Novak and Gowin, 1984). They have provided teachers with a range of learning theories and their relevance to actual teaching (Bigge, 1982; Fontana, 1984; Glynn, 1983; Riding,

1983; Stones, 1979); have presented the relationship between psychology and teaching (Francis, 1985); and have formulated learning 'rules' to foster efficient learning (McIntire, 1984).

But we may still be evolving towards a synthesis between the identified requisites and conditions for learning and the applications of theories of 'learning difficulties', which cannot finally be conceptualised differently from learning *per se*. If researchers could empirically find common premises on which to investigate teaching/learning difficulties we might yet find pragmatic solutions to many a problem that has bedevilled teachers and especially how to reach each child's teachable self and develop it to the hilt.

Finally, a word about the young learner him or herself. There was an earlier allegation in this chapter that, traditionally, children have not been encouraged to articulate their views about themselves as learners – how they see their learning assets; what are the obstacles to their learning; what best motivates them; what activities they prefer; what keeps them on or off tasks; how relevant they perceive to be the various classroom and activities in which they engage.

A start is suggested (see Assessment and Intervention above) to develop means by which children can directly be part of the corporate team approach. The extent to which children can be thus consulted will depend upon age, the degree of 'slow-learning' or developmental delay and whether or not there is a sensory handicap that precludes easy communication by conventional means. But the principle ought to be established, agreed, acted upon and solutions found to bring children fully into the collaborative processes of meeting their needs. As Nisbet and Shucksmith (1986) point out, learning in the future is likely 'to be characterised by a higher degree of independent, self-motivated learning', and we need to develop strategies 'which involve a higher level of self-monitoring than teachers have been accustomed to expect from their pupils' (pages 91, 92).

REFERENCES

*Akerman, T., Gunelt, D., Kenward, P., Leadbetter, P., Mason, L., Matthews, C. and Winteringham, D. (1983) 'DATAPAC: an interim report'. Department of Educational Psychology, Birmingham University.

Ainscow, M. and Muncey, J. (1983) Learning difficulties in the primary school, an inservice training initiative, *Remedial Education*. **18** (3) pp. 116–24.

Ainscow, M. and Muncey, J. (1984) *SNAP*. Cardiff Drake Educational Associates.

*Ainscow, M. and Tweddle, D. (1979) *Preventing Classroom Failure: an Objectives Approach*. Chichester: Wiley and Sons.

Ainscow, M. and Tweddle, D. (1984) *Early Learning Skills Analysis*. Chichester: Wiley and Sons.

Ausubel, D. (1978) *Educational Psychology, a Cognitive View*, 2nd edn. London: Holt, Rinehart and Winston.

Becker, W., Engelmann, S., Carnine, D. and Rhine, W. (1981) 'Direct instruction model', in W. Rhine (ed.) *Making Schools More Effective, New Directions from Follow-Through*. New York: Academic Press.

*Bentley, C. and Malvern, D. (1983) *Guides to Assessment in Education: Mathematics*. Basingstoke: Macmillan Education.

Bigge, M. (1982) *Learning Theories for Teachers* 4th edn. London: Harper and Row.

Bishop, M., Copley, M. and Porter, J. (eds) (1986) *Portage: More than a Teaching Programme*. Windsor: NFER-Nelson.

Bloom, B. (1983a) *All our Children Learning*. New York: McGraw Hill.

Bloom, B. (1983b) *Human Characteristics and School Learning*. New York: McGraw Hill.

Brennan, W. (1982) *Changing Special Education*. Milton Keynes, Open University Press.

*Bryans, T. and Wolfendale, S. 'Child in school profile', pilot version. Contact Trevor Bryans, L. B. Brent School Psychological Service, or Sheila Wolfendale, Psychology Department, North East London Polytechnic.

Bullock, Lord A. (Chair) (1975) *A Language for Life*. London: HMSO.

Cameron, R. J. (ed.) (1981) Issue on curriculum objectives, *Remedial Education*, **16** (4), November.

*Croll, P. and Moses, D. (1985) *One in Five: The Assessment and Incidence of Special Educational Needs*, London: Routledge and Kegan Paul.

Evans, P. (1985) 'Psychology and special educational needs: Pygmalion revisited', in H. Francis (ed.) *Learning to Teach: Psychology in Teacher Training*. Lewes: Falmer Press.

Farnham-Diggory, S. (1978) *Learning Disabilities*. London: Fontana and Open Books.

Fish, J. (1985) *Special Education: The Way Ahead*. Milton Keynes: Open University Press.

Fontana, D. (ed.) (1984) *The Education of the Young Child* 2nd edn. Oxford: Basil Blackwell.

Francis, H. (ed.) (1985) *Learning to Teach: Psychology and Teacher Training*. Lewes: Falmer Press.

Gains, C. and McNicholas, J. (ed.) (1979) *Remedial Education: Guidelines for the Future*. Harlow: Longman.

Gagné, R. (1985) *The Conditions of Learning and Theory of Instruction* 4th edn. London: Holt, Rinehart and Winston.

Galloway, D. (1985) *Schools, Pupils and Special Educational Needs*. Beckenham: Croom Helm.

Gipps, C. and Gross, H. (1984) 'LEA policies in identification and provision for children with special educational needs in ordinary schools, results from a national questionnaire survey carried out Autumn 1983',

Occasional Paper No. 3 from Screening and Special education provision in schools project, University of London Institute of Education, May.

Glynn, T. (1983) 'Building an effective teaching environment', in K. Wheldall and R. Riding (eds) *Psychological Aspects of Learning and Teaching*. Beckenham: Croom Helm.

Gulliford, R. (1985) *Teaching Children with Learning Difficulties*. Windsor: NFER-Nelson.

Hirst, P. and Peters, R. S. (1970) *The Logic of Education*. London: Routledge and Kegan Paul.

Hodgson, A., Clunies-Ross, L. and Hegarty, S. (1984) *Learning Together: Special Educational Needs in Ordinary School*, Windsor: NFER-Nelson.

*ILEA Research and Statistics Branch. 'Me at school', pilot version, part of research project.

*Indoe, D. (1986) 'Contracting using self-monitoring and self-recording with top juniors'. M.Sc. dissertation, Psychology Department, North East London Polytechnic.

*Jewell, T., Booth, S., Pollard, I., McNab, I., Rushton, A., Forrester, A. and Lindley, K. *PETSL* contact Tim Jewell, Psychology Department, North East London Polytechnic.

Jewell, T. and Feiler, A. (1985) A review of behaviourist teaching approaches in the UK, *Early Child Development and Care*, **20**, pp. 67–86.

Kail, R. (1984) *The Development of Memory in Children* 2nd edn. New York: W. H. Freeman.

Kiernan, C. (1981) *Analysis of Programmes for Teaching*. Basingstoke: Globe Education.

*Leach, D. and Raybould, T. (1977) *Learning and Behaviour Difficulties in Schools*. London: Open Books.

Lister, T. and Cameron, R. J. (1986) Curriculum Management: Planning Curriculum Objectives, *Educational Psychology in Practice*, **2** (1) April.

*Lovitt, T. (1984) *Tactics for Teaching*. Columbus, OH: Charles E. Merrill.

Matthews, C. and Booth, S. (1982) Precision teaching: or how to find out if your teaching is effective without waiting a term or even a year. *Remedial Education* **17** (1) February.

McBrien, J. (1981) Introducing the EDY project, *Special Education, Forward Trends*, **8** (2) pp. 29–36.

McCreesh, J. and Maher, A. (1974) *Remedial Education: Objectives and Techniques*. London: Ward Lock Educational.

McIntire, R. (1984) 'How children learn', in D. Fontana (ed.) *The Education of the Young Child* 2nd edn. Oxford: Basil Blackwell.

*Newson, E. and Hipgrave, T. (1982) *Getting Through to your Handicapped Child*. Cambridge: Cambridge University Press.

Nisbet, J. and Shucksmith, J. (1986) *Learning Strategies*. London: Routledge and Kegan Paul.

Novak, J. and Gowin, D. (1984) *Learning How to Learn*. Cambridge: Cambridge University Press.

Oliver, D. (1982) 'The primary curriculum: a proper basis for planning', in C. Richards (ed.) *New Directions in Primary Education*. Basingstoke: Taylor and Francis.

*Ollendick, T. and Hersen, M. (1984) *Child Behavioural Assessment, Principles and Procedures*. Oxford: Pergamon.

*Pearson, L. and Lindsay, G. (1986) *Special Needs in Primary Schools, Identification and Intervention*. Windsor: NFER-Nelson.

Potts, P. (1983) 'Summary and prospect', in T. Booth and P. Potts (eds) *Integrating Special Education*. Oxford: Basil Blackwell.

*Pumfrey, P. (1985) *Reading: Tests and Assessment Techniques* 2nd edn. Sevenoaks: Hodder and Stoughton and UKRA.

Raybould, E. (1984) 'Precision teaching', in D. Fontana (ed.) *Behaviourism and Learning Theory in Education*. Edinburgh: Scottish Academic Press for BJEP.

*Raybould, E. and Solity, J. (1985) 'Teaching with precision', in C. Smith (ed.) *New Directions in Remedial Education*. Lewes: Falmer Press and NARE.

Raymond, J. (1984) *Teaching the Child with Special Needs*. London: Ward Lock Educational.

Riding, R. (1983) 'Adapting instruction for the learner', in K. Wheldall and R. Riding (eds) *Psychological Aspects of Teaching and Learning*. Beckenham: Croom Helm.

Smith, C. (ed.) (1985) *New Directions in Remedial Education*. Lewes: Falmer Press.

Solity, J. (1984) *An Introduction to Direct Instruction*. University of Warwick, November.

*Sprick, R. (1981) *The Solution Book*, Henley-on-Thames: Science Research Associates.

*SRA (1985) *Direct Instruction: A Review*. Henley-on-Thames: Science Research Associates.

Stones, E. (1979) *Psychopedagogy, Psychological Theory and the Practice of Teaching*. London: Methuen.

Stott, D. (1978) *Helping Children with Learning Difficulties, a Diagnostic Teaching Approach*. London: Ward Lock Educational.

Strivens, J. (1981) 'Use of behaviour modification in special education: a critique', in L. Barton and S. Tomlinson (eds) *Special Education: Policy, Practice and Social Issues*. London: Harper and Row.

Swann, W. (1985) 'Psychological science and the practice of special education', in G. Claxton et al., *Psychology and Schooling: What's the Matter?* Bedford Way Papers No. 25, London University Institute of Education.

Tansley, A. and Gulliford, R. (1960) *The Education of Slow-Learning Children*. London: Routledge and Kegan Paul.

Tansley, P. and Pankhurst, J. (1981) *Children with Specific Learning Difficulties*. Windsor: NFER-Nelson.

Thomas, G. (1985) What psychology had to offer education – then, *Bulletin BPS*, **38** pp. 322–326.

*Topping, K. and Wolfendale, S. (eds) (1985) *Parental Involvement in Children's Reading*. Beckenham: Croom Helm.

Tweddle, D. and Pearson, L. (1984) 'The formulation and use of behavioural objectives', in D. Fontana (ed.) *Behaviourism and Learning Theory in Education*. Edinburgh: Scottish Academic Press for BJEP.

*Vincent, D. (1985) *Reading Tests in the Classroom*. Windsor: NFER-Nelson.

Wedell, K. (1983) Assessing special educational needs, *NUT Secondary Education Journal* **13** (2) June.

Welton, J., Wedell, K., Vorhaus, G. (1982) *Meeting Special Educational Needs; the 1981 Education Act and its Implications*, Bedford Way Papers No. 12. Tadworth: Heinemann Educational Books and Institute of Education, London University.

*Westmacott, S. and Cameron, R. J. (1981) *Behaviour Can Change*. Basingstoke: Globe Education.

Wheldall, K. (ed.) (1981) The Behaviourist in the classroom, aspects of applied behavioural analysis in British educational contexts, *Educational Review*, Offset Publications No. 1, Department of Educational Psychology, University of Birmingham.

White, D. R. and Haring, N. G. (1980) *Exceptional Teaching*. Columbus, OH: Charles E. Merrill.

*Willey, M. (1985) *A Strategy for Early Intervention in Special Needs in the Ordinary School*, Perspectives No. 15. School of Education, Exeter University, March.

Wolfendale, S. (1980) Learning difficulties: a reappraisal, *Remedial Education*, **15** (3), August.

Wolfendale, S. (1986) 'Ways of increasing parental involvement in children's development and education', in J. Harris (ed.) *Child Psychology in Action: Linking Research and Practice*. Beckenham: Croom Helm.

*Wolfendale, S. (1986) Parental contribution to Section 5 (Education Act 1981) assessment procedures, *Early Child Development and Care*, **24** (3 & 4).

Wolfendale, S. and Bryans, T. (1979) *Identification of Learning Difficulties: A Model for Intervention*. Stafford: NARE.

Wolfendale, S. and Bryans, T. (1979) *Handbook for Teachers: Suggestions for Behaviour and Learning Management*. NARE.

*Wolfendale, S. and Bryans, T. (1980) Intervening with learning in the Infant School, *Remedial Education*, **15** (1) February.

*Wood, J. (1984) *Adapting Instruction for the Mainstream*. Columbus OH: Charles E. Merrill.

4

The management of behaviour in school

Distinguishing behaviour from learning by having two separate chapters is avowedly a somewhat artificial divide; yet one that is consistent with literature on the subjects. It is unfortunate that for reasons to do with handling and processing vast amounts of information, we demarcate in this way, for it betokens a conceptual divide that does not exist in reality in or out of classrooms. Learning and motivation, self-esteem and behaviour in and out of class are inextricably bound up, as we all know. Even writers who make valiant attempts to present the interrelationship of learning and behaviour have to present separately techniques and programmes towards promoting learning, and changing and managing behaviour.

This chapter, then, has to abide by these distinctions for the purposes of discussing and presenting material within defined and delineated conceptual frameworks. However, the chapter follows on from chapter 3 deliberately, so that the links and cross-matching are evident to and easily accomplished by the reader. The structure of this chapter also bears some similarity to that of the previous chapter.

There has been a proliferation, in recent years, of texts and manuals on dealing with 'troublesome and troubling' behaviour and a number of these will be referred to and invoked in this chapter. Such a surge in the literature reflects expressed concern over the perceived prevalence of disruptive behaviour, growth of provision and the development of 'technologies' and programmes to alter and manage behaviour.

The preoccupation with 'difficult' behaviour is self-evidently due to the issues of control posed by any kind of deviant, antisocial behaviour. That is, teachers hope and expect to manage child behaviour in their classes and have expectations, as do parents, of individual behaviour and social interaction that conform to societal norms and prevailing moral codes. Lack of adherence to these norms interferes with lessons and class management in general and raises teachers' anxieties that they will not be able to teach, and that they may not have adequate strategies to avert, reduce, or change offending behaviour.

So, although in teacher training emphasis is given to setting classroom conditions to promote positive (conforming) behaviour, in reality the focus of attention and the spur of action is on preventing and coping with difficult and disturbing behaviour.

SCOPE OF THE CHAPTER

This book is about 'special' educational needs, that is to say, the distinct and identifiable 'needs' of children within schools, and how schools, in partnership with others, can devise and implement policies for ensuring that these are recognised and met. In chapter 1 the principle of the basic rights of children to these considerations was introduced. The remit of chapter 3 was to examine how children's learning needs could be provided for whereas this chapter examines how schools are organised to deal with behaviour and emotional difficulties. As importantly, it explores how schools can provide a learning and social environment that is conducive to children feeling settled, at ease, and motivated. We would all hope that children feel comfortable in school, are motivated to learn, enjoy a positive dialogue with teachers and peers, and for those under stress from other sources, find it a solace to be in school.

A prime aim of this chapter is to interrelate two major themes:
1. To present examples of recent and current work on identifying, assessing, and intervening with behaviour and emotional difficulties in primary schools.
2. To then examine how climates for positive behaviour can most effectively be created and maintained.

Towards achieving these aims, we will look at terminology and definitions, and briefly refer to concepts of aetiology and psychopathology within the context of the growth in provision for behaviour/emotional difficulties and disruptive behaviour. At the end of the chapter there will be an attempt to outline a policy on behaviour management that primary schools could adopt, within what could be termed a 'code of practice'.

ISSUES OF TERMINOLOGY AND DEFINITION

Certain terms in education have become common currency, despite expressed reservations over their continued use. The Warnock Committee examined the concept of maladjustment and professed itself to be unhappy over the label with its confused, uncertain aetiology and consequent value-laden attributes. Maladjustment is, within the parameters of the Education Act 1981, a 'grey' area, as is the issue within LEAs as to whether or not 'maladjusted', 'disturbed', 'disruptive' children should be statemented. The decisions tend to depend on existing criteria within LEAs for admission to local provision (on- and off-site units, centres, schools, even home tuition).

Terminology, not surprisingly, is confused and confusing since it mirrors the never-to-be-resolved debates about aetiology and cause and effect.

The literature reflects the search for ways to pin down, in epidemiological contexts, the elusive nature of the origins and incidence of behaviour and emotional problems. It also seeks to track down signs and symptoms of what might well be within the parameters of 'normal' social and emotional development (Rutter, Tizard and Whitmore, 1970; Shepherd, Oppenheim and Mitchell, 1971; Stott, Marston and Neill, 1975). The Warnock Report used these and other statistics, in part, to arrive at its percentage of children estimated to have special needs at any one time.

The main official category (up to the Education Act 1981) *maladjustment* has continued to vex educationalists and clinicians. Since Laslett's book (1977), which represented a theory-practice mix, there have been other books and chapters that give an examination and critique of the concept (Bowman, 1981; Stott, 1982), and Woolfe (1981) scrutinises the use of the term within the context of local authority decision making.

In order to make the label 'maladjustment' meaningful, there have been attempts to define it by listing behaviours that singly, or in combinations, have been said to be maladjusted (e.g. Underwood Report, 1955). Later, broadening the term to encompass disturbed/disturbing behaviour, and to include signs of psychiatric relevance, Rutter proposed 11 categories (1965) and Stott, Marston and Neill proposed some based on their own research (1975). Later still, Rutter (1975) put forward nine main criteria by which to gauge the extent of a child's behavioural or emotional disturbance. For the practitioner, these can be useful indices but they cannot be regarded as fixed or invariable, whether the signs and symptoms come as 'single spies' or in 'battalions' (Shakespeare – *Hamlet*).

The psychopathological literature is vast and sources used in this country are mainly, but not wholly, American. They relate survey, epidemiological, and clinical data back to aetiological behavioural and sociological, and thence to data from treatment and its results. Recommended texts are Achenbach (1982), Morris and Kratochwill (1983), Rhodes and Paul (1978), Schwartz and Johnson (1981). They and other such tomes represent valiant attempts to pin down elusive human behaviour, its conforming as well as deviant characteristics. Naturally, terms, concepts, explanations, and data from one set of theoretical constructs may not be compatible with those of another, thus the semantic confusion alluded to above is perpetuated by the existence of a number of competing frameworks, each, moreover, with differing historical origins.

Other labels have been adopted as working terms, such as 'disturbed', 'disturbing', 'troubled', 'troublesome', 'deviant', 'delinquent', 'antisocial'. The demarcation between 'neurotic' and 'conduct' disorders (Rutter, 1965) can be seen to be an attempt to neaten the semantic untidiness.

Another factor to take into account is the changing fashion in deeming aspects of behaviour to be a problem. Williams (1977) noted that teachers in the 1920s expressed concerns about children's sexual behaviour whereas nowadays they are more concerned about disruptive antisocial or aggressive behaviour. Folklore decrees that, at any one period in history, child and adolescent behaviour is alleged to be worse than at any other. The 'moral panic' (Cohen, 1972) of our contemporary times is such that media headlines scream at us that the latest survey shows that the behaviour of schoolchildren from infant school age upwards is worse and more out of control than ever. Social conformity hits no headlines!

A final comment on the fickleness of concepts and labels to do with children's behaviour that causes concern and generates emotions. Children's behaviour is invariably reported by adults and it is adults who define 'problem' behaviour. Often such judgements may be little more than reflections of arbitrary and subjective biases on the part of adults, or else of their limits of tolerance (Wolfendale and Bryans, 1979).

ISSUES OF SOCIAL CONTROL

As long as societies and communities retain notions of acceptable/ unacceptable behaviour, and devise a range of sanctions to contain, control and punish, then likewise schools and educators cannot realistically expect to find simplistic solutions to endemic and core societal and human issues. This is especially so whilst, in global terms, strife and wars are as much part of the human condition as ever they have been.

This is a preamble to acknowledging that, irrespective of the terminology we employ, and stripped of clinical and therapeutic explanations, we retain, as a bottom-line, the notion of control. Any kind of maladaptive behaviour is deviant and a departure from the inhouse rules, and social and moral codes (Hargreaves, Hester and Mellor, 1975). Teachers take very properly and seriously their ability or inability to control (to contain or redirect) the behaviour of individuals or groups.

It is arguable whether or not educational provision for disruptive children is benignly therapeutic or less than benignly controlling. Teachers may be viewed as 'friendly policemen/women' in another guise, no less agents of social control than are 'real' policemen and policewomen.

Ford, Mongon and Whelan (1982) express profound unease with the whole referral, assessment, labelling, and placement processes. They assert that even setting up such processes predisposes us to look for and find stereotypes to fit the bill, i.e., fill the provision, whether it is a local off-site unit for disruptives or a residential school for maladjusted children. They contend that special educational provision cannot simply be accepted as a demonstration of philanthropic concern for the pupils but that the use of labelling in conjunction with special education is potentially an oppressive force. They perceive that professionals who play their part in these processes are collusive and perpetuate these inherent forces.

Denis Mongon is also one of the authors of a book in this series, *Making a Difference: Teachers, Pupils and Behaviour*, in which these themes are elaborated. To that extent, this chapter is a trailer to an in-depth scrutiny of labelling, attitudes, provision, and aims to dovetail into that book. The issues raised in this chapter, and the measures proposed to combat and solve identified problems, are to be viewed as part of a primary school's overall responses and strategies towards special needs.

Whilst issues of social control may be at the heart of the matter, nevertheless, the collective responsibility, which is the central message of this book, must be predicated upon the relativities of deviant behaviour. Simplistic sets of sanctions, invoking rules, threatening disciplinary measures, have been shown merely to contain but never to solve any one school's problems of unrest and dissident behaviour. How schools can evolve coherent sets of strategies is pursued through the rest of the chapter. Alternative provision, as a backcloth and supplement to mainstream, is referred to later on.

PRIMARY SCHOOLS AS SOCIAL AND LEARNING ENVIRONMENTS: TEACHERS' CONCERNS

The term 'behaviour' has been used loosely as a 'catch all'. It refers to individual responses, interaction with the environment, social interaction in twos or in groups. It includes verbal as well as non-verbal means of communication and the interpretation of people's behavioural repertoires by other people.

Children in class and in playgrounds are continually translating social signals and cues and acting and responding accordingly – as are adults. Within schools, the social system that works in a largely self-regulatory way, with minor conflicts, demarcation disputes, misunderstandings being fairly speedily resolved, breaks down when teachers acknowledge that it is out of their direction and control and is literally unmanageable. Mostly it is individuals who challenge and upset the system, though teachers and psychologists are entirely familiar with the associated phenomenon of a corresponding rise in the social temperature of a given class.

There has been, during the last ten years, a spate of texts for teachers that aim to assist them in identifying and expressing their concerns, and thence to devising strategies for intervening. Leach and Raybould (1977) went to great pains to shift attitudes away from within-child child-deficit models (see chapter 1 of this book) to explain 'naughtiness' and nuisance behaviour, and likewise to reduce dependency on the prejudice that children who are badly behaved in class, tend to come from 'poor', 'inadequate', homes with uncaring parents or with a sole parent. They and other writers (Wolfendale and Bryans, 1979) have encouraged the redefinition of problem behaviour into descriptors, and have advanced techniques of identification and intervention that exclude and bypass the pitfalls of ascribing cause to presumed effects. Their suggested strategies include observing, describing, listing, and recording as precursors to action, whether it be individually focussed programmes (see below), group and class management (Robertson, 1981; Fontana, 1985), or emphasis on inservice and support within schools (Hanko, 1985). Yet other writers have adopted a case study format, thus providing exemplars – the principles from which practitioners can derive their own practice (Galloway, 1976; Murgatroyd, 1980; Harrop, 1983; Morgan, 1984; Merritt, 1985).

Often these texts have been a response to needs oft-expressed by teachers to have strategies for recognising and dealing with unwanted behaviour more readily available. Their concerns centre around their justifiable goal of both teaching and managing efficiently, and reconciling these goals with their responsibility to meet children's needs in school.

The section that follows draws together a number of recent and current approaches. It first examines those within behavioural frameworks since these are, to date, the most productive and consistently pragmatic.

RESPONDING TO BEHAVIOUR DIFFICULTIES

With reference to behavioural frameworks

Many of the volumes that comprise the behavioural 'stable' are manuals that present a rationale, followed by a step-by-step presentation of strategies and examples of record-keeping. Explicit in many of these is the acknowledgement that the trigger that inspires action is unwanted behaviour, though of course the longer-term goal is to create, maintain, and manage positive behaviour.

Earlier pace-setters were Poteet (1973) and Ackerman (1972) both of whom introduced the idea of situational analysis, basing measurement on observation and recording and providing an ample number of techniques to modify behaviour, build in rewards, and maintain change.

Rationales. Behaviourists cut through what they see as 'fuzzy' unclear descriptions and explanations of maladaptive behaviour and prefer to concentrate on what can be done here and now to prevent a problem worsening and to ameliorate it. Cheesman and Watts (1985) set out a ten-point charter summarising their underlying assumptions. Central to its theme is that:

- behaviour is learned
- if it has not been learned it can be taught
- most child behaviour problems are simply excess or deficits of behaviour common to all children
- learning must be within a social context
- the teacher is the most appropriate change agent within schools.

Wheldall (1983), Herbert (1981), Morgan (1984) and McGregor McMaster (1982) stake out similar principles.

Features of behavioural approaches

All advocate stringently delineated sequences of action. For example, Lane (1986) outlines these phases: definition, assessment, formulation, intervention, follow-up. The BATPACK course (The Behavioural Approach to Teaching Package, Wheldall and Merritt, 1984) consists of these units:

- identifying troublesome behaviour
- having an overview of the behavioural approach to teaching
- focussing on good behaviour; practising positives
- achieving the right classroom setting
- dealing with more troublesome behaviour

• tactics and implementation.

McGregor McMaster sets out five systematic stages: observations, definition, availability (determining the available reinforcers), deciding which to use, and action.

Behaviours to be changed

Succinctly, most behaviours are considered to be amenable to change. The literature is full of case study, single and group designs and their outcomes. Some of these have already been cited (also see the *Journal of the Association for Behaviour Approaches with Children*). Thus, no teacher or other child-carer need feel that intractable behaviour cannot be modified, no matter how severe the aggression, disruption, compulsive/obsessive acts, withdrawal, lack of cooperation, etc.

Teacher inservice training and support

A lot of the earlier behaviour modification was designed as individual, child-focussed intervention, responding to need, to children 'referred' for one reason or another. Later, as the techniques became more refined and the results of single-case treatment convincing, the methodology was developed to such a point that training could be given to teachers. Current examples of seminal inservice approaches are BATPACK (reference above) for primary schools and PAD (Preventive Approaches to Disruption, Tweddle, 1986) for secondary schools. Features of inservice training packages are that the manuals are concise, sequential, case study illustrated, with back up video and take-away material which allows for discussion, role-play, and learning by doing.

These models of INSET have been taken up and adapted for LEA use. Training courses and materials for behaviour management in schools based on behavioural approaches have been developed in, for example, the London Borough of Haringey, in Birmingham, Coventry, Leeds and Surrey. Such programmes abound in America. One American import into the United Kingdom is 'Changing Classroom Environment' PAL (Program for Affective Learning, METRA).

Limitations and Critique of Behavioural Approaches

Proponents of behavioural approaches argue that the numerous case studies of successful application of principles into practice justify the rationale and the methods. They argue that, given the brief to improve, modify behaviour by changing the conditions (introducing rewards, applying consistent sanctions, involving children directly, where possible, as self-recorders), if success results, that is sufficient justification.

However, as we saw in chapter 3, the criticism goes beyond purely pragmatic criteria to encompass moral, philosophical, social issues. Harrop (1983) in his final chapter faces up squarely to some of the issues. But even those who are uneasy about the concepts and methods and are sympathetic to attitudes discussed earlier in the chapter about schools being agencies of social control, may acknowledge that behavioural approaches can be one coherent strategy within a rather more eclectic armoury of approaches to understanding and dealing with deviant and disaffected behaviour.

With reference to other approaches

This section sub-divides, to look at within-school intervention, including referring to and co-working with support agencies, and concludes with reference to alternative provision.

Within-school

Traditionally there has been little sustained support and treatment directed at and taking place in schools, particularly primary schools. In part acknowledging this lack, one British study (Kolvin et al., 1981) aimed to identify and characterise psychiatric and educational difficulties in children and to compare different ways of helping them overcome these difficulties. Four treatment approaches, over a period of up to a couple of years, were tested: behaviour modification, nurture work, parent counselling-teacher consultations, and group therapy. Studies were made of 265 children in junior schools and 309 in secondary schools.

The best junior results were in the playgroup regime and to a lesser extent in the nurture work programme, whilst in the secondary schools the 'best' approaches were the behaviour modification and group therapy. However, the 'small-print' of this ambitious and complex study repays reading and is thought-provoking, not only about 'best treatment buys', but about the personnel support needed to sustain such programmes.

Counselling in schools has had a patchy, chequered history in Britain. It has been advocated with varying degrees of enthusiasm at different times and there are inservice courses for teachers. But there has never been the sort of take-up in British schools that has been seen in North America where counsellors on high school staffs are common. It has never been seen as a priority in resource allocation and maybe, too, there has been an unwillingness to acknowledge that behaviour and emotional problems in schools are the proper province of teachers.

Sisterson (1983) makes a case for the development of pupil counselling in primary schools and advocates the incorporation of counselling training into teacher training. In the same journal, which is on the theme of guidance and counselling, there is an attempt to regenerate interest in counsellor education. One of the authors, Raymond, has since developed ideas (1985) as to what teachers can do in primary and secondary schools about presenting problems as well as positively fostering social and life skills. She is explicit about teachers' legitimate role in the area of pastoral care. Her work, as well as that of Thacker (1985), will be used as referents in this chapter when considering constructive approaches to promoting positive behaviour.

Schools and support agencies working in co-operation

The emphasis here is on within-school action taken largely by professionals. The involvement of parents on problem definition and intervention with behaviour and emotional difficulties will be considered later.

The recent growth of co-operative endeavours has in part arisen from dissatisfaction with traditional practice, which tended to polarise emotional/behavioural problems into referrable or non-referrable and what was and was not the province of schools or other agencies such as social services, psychological services, and child guidance.

Examples of recent work that demonstrates the effectiveness of co-operation between schools and services included the support team's work in some ILEA schools (Coulby and Harper, 1985), Hanko's teacher training and support work in schools (1985), the joint systems approach of Campion (1985) and Dowling and Osborne (1985). Coulby and Harper view the provision of the support team as part of school and LEA strategy to dealing with and preventing problems.

Conoley and Conoley (1982), drawing on their teaching, research and practice, put forward a model of school consultation, the core element of which is the relationship between the consultant (educational psychologist, social worker, counsellor, for example) and teachers. Consultants give on the job training in counselling skills, and advise and support teachers in setting up counselling and management programmes.

Beyond school: referral to other agencies

Warnock saw a key facet of the teachers' role as that of recognising and identifying children's learning and behaviour problems. There has already been some discussion regarding the criteria that determine the definition of a problem. Much inservice is directed to these very issues, e.g., SNAP (see chapters 3 and 6).

Part of a teacher's skills in detecting emerging and existing problems is to recognise their severity. Many teachers say that they are not sufficiently knowledgeable about gauging severity and typology and correspondingly are uncertain as to which are appropriate referring agencies. In my previous post as an educational psychologist, we ran a course for teachers from primary and secondary schools entitled 'Criteria for Referral' that included speakers from local services describing their work. The participants perceived the value of the course as lying in the fact that they had discussed problem-recognition, how to keep situation-records, when and to whom to refer. A referral grid was introduced that was subsequently adopted by some of the schools.

The principles that can guide a school in deciding when and to whom to refer are discussed in *Identifying Children with Special Problems* (Wolfendale, 1979). Also see Rutter's criteria discussed earlier and Leach and Raybould (1977).

Teachers may or may not be kept informed as to treatment and therapy methods employed by other agencies. Family therapy has become increasingly popular and a variety of counselling approaches can be directed to one client, e.g., the child, or other members of the family (Egan, 1982; Nelson-Jones, 1983).

There are problem areas in which it is increasingly acknowledged that teachers play a key role. Child abuse and child sexual assault are examples of where a multidisciplinary approach is now seen to be vital (Porter, 1984; Parton, 1985). Inservice training and support are being offered to teachers to help them to spot signs of abuse and interference and associated stress (Elliott, 1985). Local authorities are developing inter- and across-agency procedures and codes of practice (DHSS, 1986).

Even, then, in the area of severe emotional and behavioural disturbance, where once the demarcation between school and specialist services was clear-cut, we are beginning to see increased and better contact between the services.

Alternative provision

Passing reference must be made to the provision that is made to those children who, by virtue of the severity of their disruptive behaviour, and/or emotional disturbance, are beyond being coped with in ordinary schools. Such provision is beyond the remit of this chapter (see the forthcoming book by Mongon and Hart in this series) but is a 'grey area' and needs mentioning.

The proliferation in recent years of on- and off-site units, schools and residential centres has been described and attempts have been made to evaluate their effectiveness (Galloway et al., 1982; Topping, 1983; Mortimore et al., 1983; Lloyd-Smith, 1984).

These chronicles paint a picture of confusing variability between LEAs as to criteria for admission, discharge and regime. Many LEAs have not addressed the issue as to whether or not children placed in units, but still on the roll of their mainstream schools, should have 'the protection of a statement'. It remains to be seen whether, to be consistent with policies of integration, there will be moves to provide:

- more on-site units
- better service co-ordination
- skilled support staff
- more finance to provide other back-up resources
- systems of record-keeping
- stringent monitoring of children's progress and evaluation of the effectiveness of such provision.

SHARING CONCERNS: TOWARDS COLLECTIVE RESPONSIBILITY FOR MANAGING BEHAVIOUR

A picture having been sketched of trends in provision and methods of dealing with, in the main, unwanted behaviour, attention now turns to tangible strategies primary schools could adopt. The aim is to link these recent developments, which are not widespread, with the direct, practical steps schools can take to implement a policy of collective responsibility for special needs.

As with chapter 3, it is not possible to provide exhaustive ideas within one chapter, so the emphasis will be upon key concepts which could act as a stimulus to further ideas. The parallels with chapter 3 are intentional and one of its main messages is equally applicable to this chapter – namely, 'the nub of school-based action is the relative contribution and input of several identified key people in relation to one or more children'.

In the realm of behavioural and emotional difficulties, teamwork could operate over:

- sharing concerns
- agreeing and carrying out action
- overviewing the school's provision
- generally taking collective responsibility.

It would not do to prescribe membership exactly, but, as with the area of learning difficulties, broad representation would be essential. I envisage core school and support staff, parent representation and the presence of others from supporting services.

Profiling

In chapters 1 and 3 learning profiles were introduced and discussed, and a formula advanced for compiling one for each child. Consonant with the idea of a child profile that concentrates on maximising learning and dealing with learning difficulties, the same concept can be applied to behavioural aspects in general, and particularly to identified difficulties. Apter (1982) describes the formulation of a profile within an ecological framework and gives a case-study example of an ecological profile of a 'behaviourally disordered' pupil. There are striking similarities in terms of goal setting and sequences between this approach and that described in chapter 3, which was 'home-grown' and predated Apter's publication.

Following on, then, from the exemplar in the previous chapter, the same format will be adopted, namely, singling out two major features of a child profile with reference to behavioural difficulties. These are assessment and intervention, and they are presented in tables 4.1 and 4.2 to illustrate the collective approach. As before, a key reference list is given of approaches, techniques, workable strategies. This listing is a compact way of bringing together a number of practical possibilities and is designed to save time in delving and cross checking. As with the references in chapter 3, the references cited in the following section are asterisked in the references list at the end of this chapter for readers wishing to design and carry out programmes.

PROMOTING POSITIVE BEHAVIOUR

The last section in this chapter is concerned with the broader social climate of schools, within which positive individual and group behaviour can flourish. A number of major focuses are brought together to form part of a school's overall strategy for fostering and maintaining positive relationships between peers and adults. Still within the context of teamwork, in principle it ought to be feasible for social situations, whether in classroom or playground, not to get out of hand if:

1. Personnel have identified tasks, and pre-agreed responses.
2. The response strategies are clearly seen as being part of the school's policy on behaviour management (see below).

Table 4.1 *Assessing problem behaviour: options for key people*

References key	Classteacher	Support/advisory teacher	Educational psychologists	Parents	Child
1, 2, 3, 4, 5, 6, 7, 8, 9, 10, 11, 12	Behaviour checklists; rating scales; identifying; listing concerns	←————→		'Child at Home' parental profile; observing and recording	Self-report; self-record
13, 14, 15	Personality inventories; attitude scales		←————→		

References key:
1. Galvin and Singleton (1984) **2.** Bryans and Wolfendale (1979) for the Personal Descriptive Observation sheet, also in **3.** Bryans and Wolfendale 'Child in School' profile (primary age) pilot version **4.** Leach and Raybould (1977) **5.** Coulby and Harper (1985) see Behaviour checklist (p. 69) **6.** Apter (1982) **7.** Achenbach (1985) **8.** Ollendick and Hersen (1984) **9.** Analysis of Coping Style (Boyd and Johnson 1981) **10.** Open University (1981) **11.** Westmacott and Cameron (1981) **12.** 'Parental profiling' (Wolfendale 1986) and see appendix 2 **13.** Bristol Social Adjustment Guide (Stott) **14.** ILEA 'Me at School' pilot version, see references for chapter 3 **15.** Self-reporting, see appendix 3.

Table 4.2 *Intervening with problem behaviour: options for key people (suggested framework)*

References key	Individual programmes	Group programmes	Classroom control and organisation
1, 2, 3, 4, **5, 6, 7,** **8, 9**	e.g., BATPACK SNAP	**10,** Social skills **11, 12** Life skills	**13.** Robertson (1981) **14.** TIPS (1985) **15.** Nottingham University (1980) **16.** Wood (1984) **17.** Fontana (1985)

	Work with other teachers	*Work with Support Agencies and Parents*
18	Hanko (1985)	School Psychological
19	Coulby and Harper	Service
20	Conoley and Conoley (1982)	Child Guidance
21	Wolfendale (1986)	Education Welfare Service
22	Harris (1983)	vice
23	Westmacott and Cameron (1981)	Social Services

References key:
1. BATPACK (Wheldall 1983) 2. SNAP (Coventry Special Needs Action Programme, see chapter 6) 3. Raymond (1985) 4. Cheesman and Watts (1985) 5. Walker and Shea (1984) 6. Herbert (1981) 7. Harrop (1983) 8. Sprick (1981) 9. Lovitt (1984) 10. Spence and Shepherd (1983) 11. Thacker (1985) 12. Hopson and Scally (1981).

Staff could engage in debate as to their aims for promoting positive behaviour out of which the following wishes might emerge:

- to promote social integration and ensure that children with special needs will be fully accepted in class and at play
- to provide for the development of social and life skills, either incidentally or by planned intervention

Each of these aims can be translated into medium- and longer-term objectives with corresponding programmes designed to achieve them. A few words to expand these aims follow.

Social integration. The literature on this aspect is fairly voluminous. Hegarty, who has written the foundation book to this series, *Meeting Special Needs in the Ordinary School*, writes elsewhere (1982) of findings from integration studies that the personal and social benefits to all children are manifest and long-lasting. He summarises the perceived advantages in these words:

> The school can develop and grow richer as a social institution from having a wider range of social behaviours enacted in it and a broader spectrum of relationships available to its pupils and staff. There is a symbolic component as well; the presence of pupils with special needs in a school can imply important statements about the nature of the school, its tolerance for diversity and its regard for individuals (page 104).

The notion of friendships within school is one that has hitherto received scant attention with regard to teachers actually facilitating personal and social links. We may be back to issues of social manipulation posed at the outset of the chapter. However, an espoused policy on integration must include views on how to reverse social and public attitude to handicap and disability to ensure that children with special needs have an equal niche within the mainstream of social interaction. Rubin (1980) and Hartup (1978) provide overviews on children's friendships and Asher and Gottman (1981) bring together a number of perspectives on the evolution of friendships, including that between handicapped and non-handicapped children.

Play is a related area that would be worth exploring, for as Smith (1986) points out 'it would be helpful to know more about ... whether certain forms of play provide particularly useful experience and opportunity for social skills and friendship formation' (page 13).

Social and life skills. These are areas that have burgeoned in recent years. Spence and Shepherd (1983) edited a volume that critically examined a number of programmes and their underlying rationales. These have been founded on twin tracks; firstly to make good perceived deficits in social skills, and secondly, to ensure that all children can benefit from such training.

The research still seems to be equivocal on the longer-term effectiveness. Notwithstanding what it can reveal, there have been recent moves to incorporate into or relate to the curriculum various approaches that come under the broad headings of social and life skills. Davies (1983) makes a valid distinction between these skills, though in reality it is probably difficult to demarcate clearly between social competence in handling life situations and competence in handling relationships.

Much of the work has taken place in secondary schools (David, 1983), but some of it has recently been tried out with younger children (Thacker, 1985). The work of Hopson and Scally (1981), for example, could serve as a model for adapting to primary schools, on the grounds that preparation for citizenship should start then. In terms of fostering social awareness in young children, the work of Wolfendale and Bryans (1979) provides suggestion for curriculum intervention and a pilot course is reported by Goodall et al. (no date).

WITHIN THE ECOLOGY OF THE SCHOOL

Much of the preceding discussion has concentrated on the 'micro' of dealing with individual children's behaviour, though references to classroom organisations were included on the intervention chart, table 4.2. As with learning difficulties and remediation, approaches to behaviour management have been tacked uneasily alongside the main curriculum.

A whole-school approach to learning and behaviour difficulties is increasingly seen as synonymous with meeting children's special needs. Apter's (1982) elaboration of the ecological concept fleshes out the practice of devising and implementing a through-school, within-community strategy. Fontana (1985) urges teachers to appraise their own strategies within the context of their schools' organisation. Topping (1986) casts a critical eye over the organisation sub-systems of schools that fail to build in safeguards for meeting children's needs and Pollard's title *The Social World of the Primary School* (1985) makes it explicit that schools serve a prime social function as well as being the place of learning. Pollard's thesis is that schools therefore have a responsibility to creating positive 'social worlds' for children, thus facilitating their learning.

The ecological perspective, then, embraces parental involvement. See Wolfendale (1986) for a model of a whole-school approach to behaviour management that includes parents as of right. Four levels are posited:

1. Current provision for dealing with behaviour problems.
2. The school system and current practice on involving parents.
3. School focussed INSET and identifying training needs for working with parents.
4. Direct work with parents and children.

How these four levels form a whole-school approach is explored in some detail.

A SCHOOL POLICY ON BEHAVIOUR MANAGEMENT: A CODE OF PRACTICE

To try to contain the complexity of this subject within the confines of one chapter is bound to appear glib; to attempt to define a policy for primary schools within the same chapter might merely sound presumptuous. However, this finale to the chapter is in no way intended to present a simplistic gloss to these issues. The same logic that has guided the discussion to this point underscores the recommendation for school policy, that is, it is only by concerted and co-ordinated action that schools can solve their problems and seek to evolve strategies that realise their aims.

There may be a number of identifiable requisites to as well as constraints upon the promotion of a school policy that is publishable and available to pupils, parents, governors, the LEA. Several guiding principles are offered to stimulate debate. The most that may be realistic and attainable may be for a school to explicitly acknowledge that, whilst its *code of conduct* reflects society's expectations, the rules and sanctions of an individual school are unique to that school.

That being so, it is part of the accountability of the school to publish:

- clear expectations of adherence to its rules
- its system of sanctions for each breach of rules and regulations

Pupils and parents could expect to be informed as to the system of graded differential punishments that would reflect, proportionately, the severity of the offence (often sanctions are *ad hoc*, arbitrary, and conform to no agreed code). Any lack of observance of the agreed rules would not only invoke the appropriate sanction but, as importantly, would trigger into action the agreed procedure to involve at once, the pupil concerned and his or her parents. Restoration rather than dwelling on punishment would be the cardinal goal. By this means the pupil would be enabled to be directly involved within a positive framework of jointly attempting to solve the problem, agreeing a course of action, and, most fundamentally, meeting each child's unique need.

REFERENCES

Achenbach, T. (1982) *Development Psychopathology* 2nd edn. Chichester: John Wiley and Sons.

*Achenbach, T. (1985) *Assessment and Taxonomy of Child and Adolescent Psychopathology*. Beverly Hills, CA: Sage Publications.

Ackerman, M. (1972) *Operant Conditioning Techniques for the Classroom Teacher*. Glenview, IL: Scott Foresman.

*Apter, S. (1982) *Troubled Children, Troubled Systems*. Oxford: Pergamon.

Asher, S. and Gottman, J. (eds) (1981) *The Development of Children's Friendships*. Cambridge: Cambridge University Press.

Bowman, I. (1981) 'Maladjustment: a history of the category', in W. Swann (ed.) *The Practice of Special Education*. Oxford: Basil Blackwell.

*Boyd, H. and Johnson, G. (1981) *Analysis of Coping Style, A Cognitive – Behavioural Approach to Behaviour Management*. Westerville, OH: Charles E. Merrill.

*Bryans, T. and Wolfendale, S. (1979) *Handbook for Teachers: Approaches to Learning and Behaviour Management*. Stafford: National Association for Remedial Education.

*Bryans, T. and Wolfendale, S. 'Child in school profile, primary age', pilot version (for address see chapter 3 references).

Campion, J. (1985) *The Child in Context: Family-Systems Theory in Educational Psychology*. London: Methuen.

*Cheesman, P. and Watts, D. (1985) *Positive Behaviour Management, A Manual for Teachers*. London: Croom Helm.

Cohen, S. (1972) *Folk Devils and Moral Panics*. McGibbon and Kee.

*Conoley, J. and Conoley, C. (1982) *School Consultation, A Guide to Practice and Training*. Oxford: Pergamon.

*Coulby, D. and Harper, T. (1985) *Preventing Classroom Disruption*. London: Croom Helm.

David, K. (1983) *Personal and Social Education in Secondary Schools*. London: Longman for the Schools Council.

Davies, G. (1983) An introduction to life and social skills training, *Journal of the Association of Workers for Maladjusted Children*, 1 (1), Spring.

DHSS (1986) *Child Abuse – Working Together; A Draft Guide to Arrangements for Interagency Co-operation for the Protection of Children*. DHSS April.

Dowling, E. and Osborne, E. (eds) (1985) *The Family and the School, A Joint Systems Approach to Problems with Children*. London: Routledge and Kegan Paul.

Egan, G. (1982) *The Skilled Helper*. USA: Booksco.

Elliott, M. (1985) *Preventing Child Sexual Assault, A Practical Guide to Talking with Children*. Child Assault Prevention Programme. London: Bedford Square Press.

*Fontana, D. (1985) *Classroom Control*. London: Methuen and British Psychological Society.

Ford, J., Mongon, D. and Whelan, M. (1982) *Special Education and Social Control; Invisible Disasters*. London: Routledge and Kegan Paul.

Galloway, D. (1976) *Case Studies in Classroom Management*. London: Longman.

Galloway, D., Ball, T., Blomfield, D. and Seyd, R. (1982) *Schools and Disruptive Pupils*. London: Longman.

*Galvin, P. and Singleton, R. (1981) *Behaviour Problems: A System of Management*. Windsor: NFER-Nelson.

Goodall, O., Beale, M., Beleschenko, A. and Murchison, P. (no date) *Developing Social Awareness in Young Children. A Pilot Course.* Exeter Workbooks in Education No. 4., University of Exeter.

*Hanko, G. (1985) *Special Needs in Ordinary Classrooms.* Oxford: Basil Blackwell.

Hargreaves, D., Hester, S. and Mellor, F. (1975) *Deviance in Classrooms.* London: Routledge and Kegan Paul.

*Harris, S. (1983) *Families of the Developmentally Disabled.* Oxford: Pergamon.

*Harrop, A. (1983) *Behaviour Modification in the Classroom.* London: Hodder and Stoughton.

Hartup, W. (1978) 'Children and their friends', in H. McGurk (ed.) *Issues in Childhood Social Development.* London: Methuen.

Hegarty, S. (1982) Integration and the comprehensive school, *Educational Review,* Special issue 14. Faculty of Education, University of Birmingham.

*Herbert, M. (1981) *Behavioural Treatment of Problem Children: A Practice Manual.* London: Academic Press.

*Hopson, B. and Scally, M. (1981) *Lifeskills Teaching.* London: McGraw Hill.

Kolvin, I., Garside, R. F., Nicol, A. R., Macmillan, A., Wolstenholme, F. and Leitch, I. M. (1981) *Help Starts Here – The Maladjusted Child in the Ordinary School.* London: Tavistock Publications.

Lane, D. (1986) 'Promoting positive behaviour in the classroom', in D. Tattum (ed.) *Management of Disruptive Pupil Behaviour in Schools.* Chichester: John Wiley and Sons.

Laslett, R. (1977) *Educating Maladjusted Children.* London: Crosby, Lockwood, Staples.

*Leach, D. and Raybould, E. (1977) *Learning and Behaviour Difficulties in Schools.* London: Open Books.

Lloyd-Smith, M. (1984) *Disrupted Schooling: The Growth of the Special Unit.* Murray.

*Lovitt, T. (1984) *Tactics for Teaching.* Columbus OH: Charles E. Merrill.

McGregor McMaster, J. (1982) *Methods in Social and Educational Caring.* Aldershot: Gower.

Merritt, F. (1985) *Encouragement Works Better than Punishment.* Positive Products, Faculty of Education, University of Birmingham.

METRA, 1, Beechwood Avenue, Ryton, Tyne and Wear NE40 3LX.

Morgan, R. (1984) *Behavioural Treatments with Children.* London: Heinemann.

Morris, K. and Kratochwill, T. (1983) *The Practice of Child Therapy.* Oxford: Pergamon.

Mortimore, P., Davies, J., Varlaam, A. and West, A. (1983) *Behaviour Problems in Schools, An Evaluation of Support Centres.* London: Croom Helm.

Murgatroyd, S. (ed.) (1980) *Helping the Troubled Child: Inter-Professional Case Studies.* London: Harper and Row.

Nelson-Jones, R. (1983) *Practical Counselling Skills.* London: Holt, Rinehart and Winston.

Nottingham Class Management Observation Schedule, Teacher Education Project (1980) Nottingham University School of Education.

*Ollendick, T. and Hersen, M. (1984) *Child Behavioural Assessment*. Oxford: Pergamon.

*Open University (1981) *Living with Children 5–10: A Parents' Guide*. London: Harper and Row and Open University Press.

Parton, N. (1985) *The Politics of Child Abuse*. Basingstoke: Macmillan.

Pollard, A. (1985) *The Social World of the Primary School*. Eastbourne: Holt, Rinehart and Winston.

Porter, R. (ed.) (1984) *Child Sexual Abuse Within the Family*. London: Tavistock Publications.

Poteet, J. (1973) *Behaviour Modification: A Practical Guide for Teachers*. London: University of London Press.

*Raymond, J. (1985) *Implementing Pastoral Care in Schools*. London: Croom Helm.

Rhodes, W. and Paul, J. (1978) *Emotionally Disturbed and Deviant Children*. Englewood Cliffs, NJ: Prentice-Hall.

*Robertson, J. (1981) *Effective Classroom Control*. London: Hodder and Stoughton.

Rubin, Z. (1980) *Children's Friendships*. London: Fontana.

Rutter, M. (1965) Classification and categorisation in child psychiatry, *Journal of Child Psychology and Psychiatry*. **6**, pp. 71–83.

Rutter, M. (1975) *Helping Troubled Children*. Harmondsworth: Penguin.

Rutter, M., Tizard, J. and Whitmore, K. (1970) *Education, Health and Behaviour*. Harlow: Longman.

Schwartz, S. and Johnson, J. (1981) *Psychopathology of Childhood*. Oxford: Pergamon.

Shepherd, M., Oppenheim, B. and Mitchell, S. (1971) *Childhood Behaviour and Mental Health*. London: University of London Press.

Sisterson, D. (1983) Counselling in the primary school, British Psychological Society *Education Section Review*, **7** (2).

*Spence, S. and Shepherd, G. (eds) (1983) *Development in Social Skills Training*. London: Academic Press.

*Sprick, R. (1981) *The Solution Book*. Henley-on-Thames: Science Research Associates.

Smith, P. (ed.) (1986) *Children's Play: Research Developments and Practical Applications*. London: Gordon and Breach Science Publishers.

*Stott, D. (1982) *Helping the Maladjusted Child*. Milton Keynes: Open University Press.

Stott, D., Marston, N. and Neill, S. (1975) *Taxonomy of Behaviour Disturbance*. London: University of London Press.

*Thacker, J. (1985) Extending developmental groupwork to junior/middle schools: an Exeter project, *Pastoral Care*. February.

*TIPS, *The Macmillan Teacher Information Pack* (1985) Dawson, R. et al. Basingstoke: Macmillan Education.

Topping, K. (1983) *Educational Systems for Disruptive Adolescents*. London: Croom Helm.

Topping, K. (1986) 'Consultative enhancement of school-based action', in Tattum, D. (ed.) *Management of Disruptive Pupil Behaviour In Schools*. Chichester: John Wiley and Sons.

Tweddle, D. (ed.) (1986) *Preventive Approaches to Disruption*. Basingstoke: Macmillan.

Underwood Report (1955) *Report of the Committee on Maladjusted Children*. London: HMSO.

*Walker, J. and Shea, T. (1984) *Behavior Management, A Practical Approach for Educators*. St. Louis, MO: C. V. Mosby.

*Westmacott, E. V. S. and Cameron, R. J. (1981) *Behaviour Can Change*. Basingstoke: Globe Education.

*Wheldall, K. (1983) 'A positive approach to classroom discipline', in K. Wheldall and R. Riding (eds) *Psychological Aspects of Learning and Teaching*. London: Croom Helm.

Wheldall, K. and Merritt, C. (1984) BATPACK, Positive Products. Birmingham: Birmingham University.

Williams, P. (1977) *Children and Psychologists*. London: Hodder and Stoughton.

Wolfendale, S. (1979) *Identifying Children with Special Problems: Reading and Individual Development*, Action research projects, p. 234. Milton Keynes: Open University Press.

*Wolfendale, S. (1986) Parental contribution to Section 5 (Education Act 1981) assessment procedures, *Early Child Development and Care* 24 (3 and 4).

*Wolfendale, S. (1986) Involving parents in behaviour managements, a whole-school approach, *Support for Learning*, 1 (4), November.

Wolfendale, S. and Bryans, T. (1979) *Identification of Learning Difficulties: a Model for Intervention*. Stafford: NARE.

*Wood, J. (1984) *Adopting Instruction for the Mainstream*. Columbus, OH: Charles E. Merrill.

Woolfe, R. (1981) 'Maladjustment in the context of local authority decision-making', in L. Barton, and S. Tomlinson (eds) *Special Education: Policy, Practice and Social Issues*. London: Harper and Row.

5

Organisation of classroom and school: collective responsibility in action

The potential of teamwork where expertise within primary schools is harnessed towards collectively providing for special needs has been mentioned at strategic points in previous chapters. This chapter deals with the various components of teamwork and liaison and selects a number of key angles or facets to demonstrate different responsibilities intrinsic to teamwork. These will include:

- the classroom
- curriculum
- staffing
- links with special schools
- liaison with support services
- liaison with parents, and governors.

Overall, it is the vision of a network of educational and support services to meet special educational needs that guides and informs the chapter.

THE SCHOOL AS A SYSTEM

Increasing attention is being paid to the features, both abstract and concrete, that comprise and define any institution. It is acknowledged that buildings, space, room layout (visible features), as well as personnel deployment, interaction between personnel, hierarchies, communication links, organisation (less immediately visible features) are profoundly influential upon the efficient working of any institution or organisation.

Borrowing some basic concepts from engineering, several educational psychologists in the United Kingdom have described the application of systems approaches to their work in schools (Burden, 1981). It is increasingly common for educational psychologists to broaden the base of their practice by examining the 'system' and 'sub-systems' of a school in order to understand the contexts in which children find themselves daily (Figg and Ross, 1981). One of the central themes in head teachers' management training is, of course, organisation and management of the whole school. This necessitates taking a total or 'macro' perspective and applying a number of techniques, including diagrammatic, to help depict, describe, and explain the complex networks that comprise an organisation.

We shall see in this chapter that current writings within the field of special needs embrace these broader perspectives and acknowledge that it is essential to explore them in planning and managing school-based special needs provision as the 'micro' aspects of individual children's progress.

ECOLOGICAL PERSPECTIVES AND APPLICATIONS

Reference has already been made in chapter 2 to ecological perspectives that have conceptual links with systems approaches. The work has mostly been American, though there is a British book in preparation (Feiler and Thomas).

Appendix 5 contains a description of ecological intervention, the technique of 'ecomapping', provides several examples, and gives references for further reading. The potential of these approaches as part of broad-based assessment, which includes contributions from significant people in a child's life, including him or herself, has not yet been explored in any depth in Britain. One example where it is being explored, within a social services context, is described in appendix 5.

TEAMWORK

The introductory discussion above illuminates some principles of co-operative working. These principles are now outlined in general terms.

Collective responsibility for meeting children's learning and other needs in primary settings will be executed by different personnel, singly or in combinations, at any one time. Duties of key members of a designated team will doubtless be allocated as an integral part of a school's special needs policy (see chapter 7); yet it is important for all members of staff of any one school to:

- acknowledge the Warnock Report view that at any one time in any class there will be several children with special educational

needs (⅕ is, of course, the notional average based on survey evidence)
- accept their individual responsibility towards meeting children's special needs.

The discussion in chapter 1 aimed to represent what appears to be a growing consensus that the educational needs of some children are not best served by a siphoning-off of teaching expertise into remedial spheres that are kept segregated from mainstream curriculum and the hub of school activity. Since designated special needs (see chapter 1 for definitions) cannot and should not be viewed in isolation from all children's distinctive learning and other needs, it follows that all teachers have to maintain some surveillance of whether these are being met.

The all encompassing philosophy of the 'whole-school' approach to integration is examined by Thomas and Jackson (1986). Their article does not minimise what is involved in working towards organisational change at this 'macro' level. This chapter now aims to explore selected areas of teamwork and to look at current views as to how collective responsibility can work in practice.

Readers who want case study examples of teamwork in operation within integrated settings can find these described in more detail in Hegarty, Pocklington and Lucas (1982) in the appendix of Booth and Potts (1983), in Hodgson, Clunies-Ross and Hegarty (1984) and in the factsheets published by the Centre for Studies on Integration in Education (address in references).

PLANNING AND MANAGING THE CURRICULUM

Specific responsibilities for subject areas, e.g., literacy, numeracy, primary science, music, art and craft, drama, PE and others, may or may not be within the generic remit of class teachers and/or subject specialists or responsibility posts in any one primary school. However, as the Fish Report (1985) points out, 'A school's curriculum, derived from the agreed aims of the school, should reflect the cultural, social and racial diversity of the pupils who attend it and the community it serves', (page 57, para 2.7.7.).

Therefore, the collective responsibility of all the teachers within the school is to 'have a clear idea of progression in all aspects of the curriculum and to use this as a framework for evaluating individual progress' (page 57, 2.7.6.).

The Report continues

> It is on this basis for assessing the progress of all children that it is possible to become aware of children who have special educational

needs, either because they are making no progress or because their progress is significantly less than that of other children.
(page 57, 2.7.6.)

The setting of teaching objectives for each child follows within this model of a 'curriculum framework'. Echoing the particular theme of this chapter (in this book) the Fish Report goes on later to affirm in discussing curriculum

in the organisation and management of a wide range of activities including team teaching and collaborative learning are an essential basis for meeting the variety of individual needs of children in primary schools.
(page 184, 3. 17. 21.)

In chapter 1 of this book a theoretical stance was first sketched out that sought to achieve a rapprochement betwen 'good' (tried and true?) principles of primary practice and 'best' or proven practice within remedial/special education.

Some of the proven, effective features of primary curriculum practice quoted by Fish and his colleagues in chapter 7 appear to be synonymous with 'good' teaching practice in the area of special needs. Should we be surprised? Perhaps now, after creating and then nurturing red herrings in the form of segregated provision, we are rediscovering that some sound pedagogical principles do apply to all children. As we shall see below, the ORACLE researchers uncovered some factors that appeared to make for effective teaching/learning. They went on to make recommendations that would, they felt, benefit all the children within any one class with a broad spread of individual competence and a variety of 'special' learning needs.

Textbooks on primary curriculum, content and method, have traditionally dealt with all children, simply by not explicitly categorising groups of children. It may now be timely to return to these texts on behalf of those children with designated special needs – a child on a statement of special needs; one with sensory handicap, or with moderate learning difficulties; a child with epilepsy on controlled medication and under nursing surveillance; a child with a cluster of conditions needing especial attention. Campbell (1985) in fact discusses the notion of collective responsibility in staking out the territory for his book in these words

if teachers participate in some explicitly collaborative action to recreate the curriculum in their school, rather than acting as individuals to receive it, they may move closer to accepting collective

responsibility for the curriculum overall in the school, as well as for its application in their own classrooms.
(page 3)

Campbell goes on to set out his vision of the 'collegial' primary school which, he avers, is 'a projection from empirical reality' not a description of it at present. His views represent an ideal that is strikingly akin to the model of collective responsibility for special and all needs contained in this book. Campbell's 'collegial' model is predicted on the two values of 'teacher collaboration and subject expertise' (page 152).

Turning now to another contemporary text on primary education, we can see that Alexander (1984) justifies his attention to the teacher's role thus:

> because it is the teacher ... who defines the child in child-centred ... approach, who defines children's attributes, states what their needs are, predicts their potential and evaluates their achievement. It could be argued, then, that knowing oneself as a teacher is one of the basic prerequisites for true child-centredness.
> (page 2)

Here the child-centred view of primary education is reaffirmed but Alexander goes on to examine a fallacy concerned with child-centred education, namely that it has to be exclusively focussed on the child. He examines the feasibility of a 'child-centred' primary curriculum that is rooted within societal perspectives (Stonier, 1982) and says 'using societal analysis as the starting point he [Stonier] effectively avoids the individual/society polarisation which inevitably ensues from the exclusively child-centred position' (page 33).

Alexander's analysis of the curriculum has much to offer anyone coming from the direction of remedial/special education who wishes to embrace the broadest possible conception of integration. His critique of many conventional assumptions and received wisdom within education are a wincing reminder that segregated philosophies are morally untenable. Further, his view accords with this author's that the whole psycho-pedagogical basis of teacher's 'knowledge' of children, of their learning potential, their unique circumstances, needs to be challenged.

Uncomfortably, it has to be acknowledged that we are practising, thinking, writing at a time when our own knowledge of theory and practice application is still woefully inadequate.

The ideas put forward in chapters 3 and 4 of this book do represent what we think we know at the present time about how to meet children's learning needs and deal with emotional development and social adjustment. But there is much work to be done still to reconcile individual teaching approaches with theories of pedagogy that can actually be empirically tested and proven.

My aspiration, then, is to effect a synthesis between the traditions of primary and remedial/special education. In itself this could be a static aim, one that does not move us on far enough to cope with education imperatives of the 1990s and beyond. However, the fusion that is envisaged is actually to be able to offer curricula of relevance to all children – who collectively come from and represent a diversity of cultural, religious, and ethnic backgrounds. Thus, the moral imperative in Alexander's words, is 'that curriculum discourse ought to incorporate and synthesize perspectives on children, knowledge, culture and pedagogy' (page 47).

Maybe these lofty aspirations should guide our current practice, which in the meantime has to absorb a number of realities that are the legacy from a century and more of steady growth of separatist education. Part of the legacy are ambivalent attitudes on the part of teachers towards handicap and disability (Gipps and Gross, 1985; Croll and Moses, 1985; Thompson and Arora, 1985). Swann (1983) in an examination of curriculum principles for integration acknowledges these realities; his own blueprint specifies a curriculum model that incorporates elements to eliminate prejudice.

CLASSROOM ORGANISATION AND STAFFING

It is clear from contemporary texts on primary education as well as from trends in thinking in special needs that the view is increasingly disfavoured that the class teacher should be expected to shoulder the daily and entire responsibility for curriculum planning, execution and management; and that one person is capable of providing a total educational experience for all the children in his or her charge. The dangers of looking inward, what Alexander describes as the 'cosy, privatised equilibrium of "my class" (page 215) and the commensurate guilt at not achieving self-directed personal teaching goals, can be averted or at least reduced by undertaking 'collective analysis of shared issues and problems' (Alexander, 1984, page 216).

The co-operative team approach can nowhere be better put into effect than in classrooms and there is increasing evidence that corporate teaching can be the most effective way of ensuring that each child receives his or her rightful share of teacher's attention and teaching time, working solo, in combinations, in small groups in the whole class.

The question of how best to organise children within the

classroom has always attracted debate but with little corresponding empirical evidence as to prevailing custom, beyond anecdote or faulty impressionistic data (Plowden Report 1967, reference in chapter 1).

The ORACLE study (Galton, Simon and Croll, 1980; Galton and Simon, 1980) provides harder data, from which the researchers conclude 'that the whole issue of the purpose and organisation of group work in the primary school classroom requires a great deal more attention than it has had to date' (Galton et al., page 161).

It seems that there is more potential for effective learning through small group collaboration than has yet been fully realised for the evidence suggests that, within the small-group clusters so characteristic of primary classrooms, children tended to work on their own, in parallel rather than in co-operation. A recent study aimed to explore some of the most important factors behind successful group work in primary schools with a view to highlighting priorities for devising an INSET package (Crombie, 1986). Early results suggest that the INSET priorities for organisation, presentation, and the seatwork have been found to be:

Organisation. The ready availability and clearing away of materials; the setting of acceptable noise levels.

Presentation. Encouraging children to respond to statements made by peers; preventing children from talking whilst another child is speaking.

Seatwork. Dealing with two or more matters simultaneously; being aware of the behaviour of all children in the class.

There are implications here for peer tutoring, which has already been explored in the realm of reading (Crombie, also other contributors to the *Paired Reading Bulletin*, 1986); see Hodgson et al. (1984).

The planning requisites that such studies identify raise questions about staff–pupil ratios as well as the underlying issues previously raised concerning sharing responsibility. Galton, Simon and Croll (1980) are of the opinion that maximum class size in British primary schools should be 20; this number would allow for effective reaching of all the children in a truly mixed ability class and would promote co-operative learning.

Cohering with these research findings are those of special needs–focussed investigations into classroom organisation and staff deployment.

ROOM MANAGEMENT

The area of severe learning difficulties has been a pacesetter in demonstrating the effectiveness of 'room management' (RM) techniques via the provision of other staff in one classroom, each of whom have explicit jobs for an agreed period of time during a day (McBrien and Weightman, 1980; Farrell, 1985). During this 'activity' period, which could be about an hour long, specific roles are allotted to staff in the classroom:

1. *Individual helper* who concentrates on taking individual children for short periods of time.
2. *Activity manager* who looks after the work of the rest of the children, the aim being to keep the children engaged on the task in hand.
3. *Mover* who aims to maintain flow in the classroom by relieving the activity manager and individual helper from distracting events. The mover can deal with the various contingencies that crop up – coping with interruptions, sharpening pencils.

The EDY (Education of the Developmentally Young) staff training programme, which pioneered RM techniques in the United Kingdom, derives from behavioural principles, is very stringent and requires a several-day training course with certification at the end. Thousands of staff from special schools have now been trained in EDY techniques and, as with PORTAGE (see chapter 3), success can be measured by children's productivity. Children's output within EDY would be one of the criteria for gauging how effective this kind of time and motion can be.

Although the staff–pupil ratios are far higher in special schools, there are nevertheless implications for the adoption of RM techniques in mainstream schools that bear examination. Thomas (1985) considered the deployment of additional personnel, including volunteers, and in one primary school tried out the effectiveness of allotting RM roles (see above) to two parents and one ancillary helper. He acknowledges methodological and other limitations to his study, yet concludes 'the results obtained are attributable mainly to the advantages of RM accruing from specification of role'.

How realistic would it be to envisage an RM type of approach within primary classrooms, so that each child receives some structured, intensive teaching and support during a school day? In principle there seem to be evident pedagogic advantages in having extra personnel with clearly identified tasks who would corporately bring about learning gains by:

- giving immediate feedback, knowledge of results
- swiftly applying correction procedures to 'errors'

- promptly reiterating instructions
- facilitating self-monitoring by pupils
- ensuring that short-term sessional or daily goals are met
- redirecting pupils to alternative or related tasks
- flexibly matching materials and resources to child
- anticipating and dealing with behaviour
- maintaining motivation and on-task behaviour by frequent attention, interest, encouragement, and support

The physical aspects of classroom management are important corollaries of human management, such as arrangement of furniture, acoustics, lighting (Hodgson et al., 1984, chapter 10), organising the 'learning station' (Wood, 1984), and seating arrangements (Stratford). Whilst these may seem rather obvious considerations, the point here is that these too have to be articulated and worked into an overall plan of classroom management.

STAFFING AND SUPPORT

Galton et al. (see above) are unequivocal in their opinion that children should have a better deal in terms of teachers' attention. Readers are reminded that in chapter 3 of this book Bloom's five Alterable Variables were listed *vis-à-vis* their applicability in primary classrooms. In particular, number 1, 'Available time versus time-on-task', and number 4, 'Teachers versus teaching', are compatible with the view that, at present, class teachers do not have enough opportunities to utilise sound instructional principles and by virtue of having large groups have to teach in a blunt, undifferentiated way. Even when they work with small groups, teachers frequently have to attend to many other distractions in the classroom.

Booth (1983) describes the deployment of 'remedial specialists' in the Grampian region who act as consultants to other members of staff and who also work alongside the class teacher. Ferguson and Adams (1985) assess the advantages and limitations of the Grampian scheme. They are conscious of the drawbacks associated with maintaining the term 'remedial', acknowledge that we are still very much in an evolving situation, and suggest

> one way … is to make provision for both to work in the same classroom at the same time. This is a potentially useful way of integrating remedial education with the school curriculum … helping class and remedial teachers to improve their understanding of each other's problems and special skills.
> (page 99)

Fish (1985) mentions the Swedish approach to collaborative teaching as a form of team teaching. Arising from the ORACLE data (see above) it was inevitable that the authors should query whether or not team teaching in this country has ever been fully taken up and evaluated.

Hodgson et al. cite schools (without naming them) in the NFER study that utilised second teachers and ancillaries to provide support in mainstream classes, working perhaps with one pupil (possibly a child whose statement of needs explicitly calls for extra teaching help and prescribes the extent and nature of that help); with small groups of designated special needs children; with mixed groups. A useful summary of this part of the NFER study is provided by Clunies-Ross (1984).

Hockley (1985) gives a firsthand account of having been a support teacher in primary and secondary settings, and identifies and explains these elements of the classroom-based aspects of her role: flexibility; observation; problem classification and suggestions for different approaches; monitoring; consultations with staff.

The label of 'support teacher' may not be the most appropriate one to use – Hart (1986) points out that the term might imply a less than equal relationship with support ancillary to real specialists and, further, perpetuate the idea of 'remedial' being tangential to the body of the curriculum. She goes on to suggest that a broader definition of special educational need to encompass prevention would validly allow support teachers to work with other teachers to develop a curriculum 'capable of meeting a progressively wider diversity of needs' (page 58). Thus, support teachers could play a significant part in 'promoting good teaching for all children within the general curriculum', and 'working in partnership with subject teachers, support teachers could ... try out a variety of different approaches and monitor their effectiveness in catering for all needs within the class.

The Inner London Education Authority's IBIS (Inspectors Based in Schools) scheme, begun in 1986, is designed to eliminate the demarcation between ordinary and special/remedial education by giving a brief to each school-based inspector to 'help to improve the quality of education and the achievement of pupils'.

In a discussion on an INSET course with several designated 'special needs' teachers in primary schools, the teachers identified their 'whole-school' responsibilities, major elements of which included, for example, environmental studies, AVA, library, PE. Their special needs-focussed work included observation, planning and executing individual programmes of work, record-keeping, liaison, inservice with colleagues. They felt that effecting attitude-change by their colleagues was an integral part of their work.

It was clear that generic school duties were seen as concomitant with the post, and whilst this is in keeping with the spirit of integration it would be vital not to erode the specialist function of their role. Not an easy balance to maintain.

The increasing numbers of often erstwhile 'remedial', now termed 'special needs co-ordinators', etc. (see chapter 1) with this support and consultative role attests to the need for such staff deployment, but such developments are still too new for reasonable evaluation to have been made.

Finally, in this section on classroom-based personnel, a word about using parents as volunteer 'aides'. The potential of parental assistance within schools has been explored in the area of reading (see chapter 2), but far less in other curriculum areas. Without abusing their goodwill and the limited amount of time parents can offer, it would be part of the notion of collective responsibility to approach and negotiate with parents as to what they could contribute – working with groups on reading, language, maths workshops and other curriculum areas; acting as an identified 'helper' as in the RM model; providing one-to-one assistance on an individual teaching programme for a child whose statement of needs prescribes clear teaching and learning objectives. 'Parents as educators' can then become reality.

UNITS WITHIN SCHOOLS

The above discussion has concentrated on co-operative teaching within children's 'home-base', their classrooms, since, as the diagrammatic web (see page 96) shows, integration is rooted within classrooms. Much has been written on varieties of integration, though purists would maintain that any form of withdrawal is an erosion of interaction principles. If a school can demonstrate that all the children in a given class receive instruction at some time outside the classroom (which of course they do) and can thereby prove that no child or group is singled out and stigmatised in this way, then withdrawal to units, resource areas, etc. is tenable.

The reason for making reference to provision that supplements, rather than supplants, mainline classroom-based teaching is that, again, it is a requisite of pre-planned teamwork that access to specialist equipment, other resources and materials is effected on the basis of stringently defined criteria. The summary of the NFER study (Hodgson, Clunies-Ross and Hegarty, 1985) presupposes in fact that, in order to meet the special needs of children with particular disabilities, there has to be access to specialist teaching and equipment (see below).

Literature from the Warnock Report onwards, and including the NFER studies, shows variations on the theme of integration in terms of units and withdrawal arrangements. Changing practice is encapsulated by Selfe and Gray (1985) who, in describing their experience of unit provision within one rural area of a large county, aver that units within school provision is en route towards full functional integration. 'They are, in fact, better placed ... than are segregated special schools since opportunities for integration and a wider curriculum are on hand' (page 123).

Teachers are not, then, in a position to 'disown' children with special needs or their responsibility towards them and they have the opportunity to broaden their own expertise.

LINKS BETWEEN MAINSTREAM AND SPECIAL SCHOOLS

Despite official commitment to integration enshrined in the 1981 Education Act, there is no consensus as to how to implement it nor an agreed timescale. It has become evident, since the Act came into force on 1st April 1983, that LEAs vary enormously in their thinking and practice. Most do not have a written policy (see chapter 7), many do not even provide a written account of their plans, some are still deliberating via working parties and consultative documents.

And yet, on the ground, professional staff are directly responding to the Act, and ensuring that the demarcation between remedial/special/mainstream is increasingly blurred, as Warnock recommended (see chapter 1).

Since many of the links between mainstream and special schools are occurring at practitioner level, mostly routinely within LEAs, documentation chronicling these developments is inadequate. However, whilst detailed survey evidence is lacking, the literature does provide some portents as to trends and how these arrangements may work. There are a few prescriptions (Brennan, 1982) and documented examples (Hallmark and Dessent, 1982; Hallmark, 1983).

As with units-within-school provision, mainstream–special school liaison may in time be seen to have been a transitional arrangement en route to integration. But what is not and cannot yet be resolved on financial as well as ideological grounds is whether or not special schools will wither away, will become resource centres of expertise and technology, transporting them to mainstream (Dessent, 1984; Dodman, 1985), or will be retained to provide for 'special care' children.

So what we can know in the short term, pragmatically, is how special/mainstream links can meet children's needs, can rationalise local resources, can ensure sharing and pooling knowledge and concern on behalf of children. In other words, collective responsibility extends beyond the frontiers of any one school, as figure 5.1 illustrates.

In the longer term, we have to know, on the basis of evaluating the data that is accumulating now, just which aspects of these links, are especially effective. NFER is currently engaged in such a study (Moses, 1985). The CLASSIC ('Curriculum link and special schools in the community', Sigston, Kerfoot and Hogg, 1986) action-research pilot project in the London Borough of Barking and Dagenham is one of the few examples of an attempt to implement a curriculum-focussed liaison whilst concurrently evaluating process and product. The scheme is based on a well-articulated theoretical model utilising a team structure to support the curriculum and individual child programme components along the lines of 'who does what, for how long' job specification.

SCHOOLS AND SUPPORT SERVICES

The viability of various forms of working links between school staff and those from supporting agencies is currently generating interest. A recurring theme in this volume is the need for people who work with and on behalf of children to understand the bases and intentions of each other's contribution. Multidisciplinary teamwork is seen to be one of the cornerstones of the 1981 Education Act as well as being within the broader context of special needs (circular 1/83).

There are examples of inservice training organised by DHA (District Health Authority) personnel directed to teachers to acquaint them with the medical and physical implications of disability. Likewise there are courses run by LEA personnel for others in health and social services in the 1981 Education Act and educational aspects of special needs.

Courses and workshops for parents and professionals provide a forum for interdisciplinary acquaintance to be made which can lead to joint work. PORTAGE has provided opportunities for professionals who never worked together previously to interact and pool their expertise.

Again, then, on the ground we find evidence of developing networks of communication between agencies, some of these confounding the critics who are pessimistic about the ease with which professionals can divest themselves of their *amour propre*, relinquish some of their mystique, and bring their arcane jargon and rituals to public scrutiny (Potts, 1985).

The context for this chapter is the school. Teachers have the right to be far better informed about the relative contributions of the support services. That right is a prerequisite to the formulation of school-based referral procedures and liaison mechanisms. Quicke (1985) expresses the view that support should be defined in terms of mutuality, that is 'genuine teamwork implies mutual not one-way support' (page 122). Thomson's helpful list of agencies (1984) was generated as part of a study he made into the special school head teacher's position as a member of a multidisciplinary team which endorses Quicke's notion of mutuality.

Current descriptions of support services, including critiques such as Pott's own trenchant offering (1985), still take a profession-centric standpoint, tending to ignore the contribution of local and national voluntary agencies. Two exceptions are Gliedman and Roth (1981) and Adams (1986), who clearly perceive that a truly integrated child support system that includes schools is truly community-based and involves parents as equals (Wolfendale, 1983, chapters 8 and 10).

SCHOOLS, THEIR GOVERNING BODIES AND SPECIAL EDUCATIONAL NEEDS

Reference was made in chapter 2 to the particular duties school governors now have towards special needs. Based in part on experience of participating in LEA-provided governor training, I am of the opinion that there has to be a whole-school responsibility for curriculum, staff appointments, etc. in which governors, with their recently-defined responsibilities for special educational needs, play a full part.

Without a proper and informed debate taking place at local level about integration, what it means, how it could work, what the LEA is doing to promote integration, then, in lay governors' minds particularly, a demarcation of ordinary/special is likely to persist.

The provision of governor training is, anyhow, patchy and uneven, and ranges from imaginative LEA-inspired collaborative inservice, to sparse, one-off days, to nothing at all in some areas (George, 1984). Special needs as a distinct topic was not included in the Open University Training Handbook 'Governing Schools', although, if a second edition is ever produced, that omission will doubtless be rectified in the light of the legislation (Education Act 1981).

In fact, special needs are barely referred to in the various booklets for governors put out by ACE and CASE (see references), though governors can be directed to the excellent summary of the Education Act 1981 published by ACE, and in one of the ACE pamphlets *Questions Governors Ask* there is one question and answer on governors' duties towards special needs.

Bailey (1984) examines the role of governors of special schools and his analysis provides some pointers for mainstream governors. The fullest exposition to date, though, remains Paper No. 5 'Governors and special educational needs' produced by NAGM (National Association of Governors and Managers) which sets out their legal duties and provides a comprehensive checklist of questions governors ought to be asking about staffing, curricula, resources, links with other services and the community relations with parents and pupils, and disciplinary procedures. Three important new duties are assigned to governors under the 1981 Education Act. These are to:

1. Use their best endeavours to ensure that children with special needs in their schools are receiving an education that caters for them properly.
2. Ensure that everyone teaching children identified as having special needs knows about these needs and how they are to be met.
3. Ensure that everyone in schools understands the importance of identifying children with special needs and providing for them.

The Inner London branch of NAGM held a day conference on governors and special educational needs during 1985. The report (available from NAGM, see references) could provide a model of how to present special needs within a discussion and training format and in a context of integrated education. Participants included governors, parents, teachers and LEA officers, thus demonstrating collective responsibility in action.

THE NETWORK OF SERVICES

The tables contained in chapters 3 and 4 were intended to provide a summary of possibilities for joint working between class teachers, support and advisory teachers, psychologists, parents, and others. The details given in those two charts centred on assessment and intervention approaches that were considered to be amenable to co-operation. One further general example, that of ecological assessment and intervention (ecosystems and ecomapping), was given at the beginning of this chapter to further emphasise such possibilities.

Below, figure 5.1 is an illustration providing, in circular 'web' form, a representation of the network of services with which this chapter has been concerned. It therefore summarises the elements, in human terms, of collective responsibility.

A number of other contemporary texts echo the theme of co-operation, teamwork, and whole-school approach (Sayer, 1985; Thomas and Jackson, 1986). Adams (1986) provides an endorsement of the diagrammatic summary of figure 5.1 in these words: 'to operate effectively the schools should be at the centre of a network of partnerships' (page 191) and in the words of Dessent (1983)

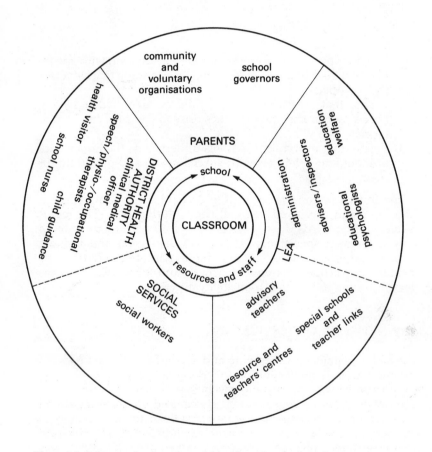

Figure 5.1 Primary schools and special needs: network of services

The challenge for the future is the development of a carefully balanced sharing of responsibility between mainstream and special staff which maximises the children's access to and opportunities within normal schools.
(page 99)

How responsibilities can be deployed will be further explored in chapter 7.

REFERENCES

ACE (Advisory Centre for Education): booklets by Joan Sallis (i) *Questions Governors Ask* (ii) *Working Together, Training Exercises* (iii) *The School in Its Setting* (iv) *The Effective School Governor*. 18 Victoria Park Square, London. E2.

Adams, F. (ed.) (1986) *Special Education*. Society of Education Officers, Harlow: Longman Group.

Alexander, R. (1984) *Primary Teaching*. London: Holt, Rinehart and Winston.

Apter, S. (1982) *Troubled Children, Troubled Systems*. Oxford: Pergamon.

Bailey, T. (1984) 'Governors and the special schools', in A. Bowers (ed.) *Management and the Special School*. Beckenham: Croom Helm.

Booth, T. (1983) 'Integrating special education', in T. Booth and P. Potts (eds) *Integrating Special Education*. Oxford: Basil Blackwell.

Brennan, W. (1982) *Changing Special Education*. Milton Keynes: Open University Press.

Bronfenbrenner, U. (1979) *The Ecology of Human Development, Experiments by Nature and Design*. Cambridge MA: Harvard University Press.

Burden, R. (1981) 'System theory and its relevance to schools', in B. Gillham (ed.) *Problem Behaviour in the Secondary School*. Beckenham: Croom Helm.

Campbell, R. J. (1985) *Developing the Primary School Curriculum*. London: Holt, Rinehart and Winston.

CASE (Campaign for the Advancement of State Education) (1985) *A Guide for New Parent Governors*. Redbridge: Redbridge CASE, October.

Clunies-Ross, L. (1984) Supporting the mainstream teacher, *British Journal of Special Education*, **11** (3), September.

Croll, P. and Moses, D. (1985) *One in Five: The Assessment and Incidence of Special Educational Needs*. London: Routledge and Kegan Paul.

Crombie, R. (1986) 'Effectively grouping primary age children', unpublished MSc dissertation, Psychology Department, North East London Polytechnic, in association with Dr. Tim Lowe, Essex School Psychological Service.

CSIE (Centre for Studies on Integration in Education), 840 Brighton Road, Purley, Croydon CR0 2BH. Tel. 01-660-8552.

DES Circular 1/83 *Assessments and Statements of Special Educational Needs* 31st January.

Dessent, A. (1983) 'Who is responsible for children with special needs?', in A. Booth and P. Potts (eds) *Integrating Special Education*. Oxford: Basil Blackwell.

Dessent, A. (1984) 'Special schools and the mainstream', in A. Bowers (ed.) *Management and the Special School*. Beckenham: Croom Helm.

Dodman, M. (1985) Delivering support services to mainstream schools: a role for the special school, *Perspectives 15*. School of Education, Exeter University.

Farrell, P. (1985) *EDY: Its Impact on Staff Training in Mental Handicap*. Manchester: Manchester University Press.

Feiler, A. and Thomas, G. (eds) (in prep.) *Meeting Special Needs: An Ecological Perspective*. Oxford: Basil Blackwell.

Ferguson, N. and Adams, M. (1985) 'Assessing the advantages of team teaching in remedial education: the remedial teacher's role, in C. Smith (ed.) *New Directions in Remedial Education*. Brighton: Falmer Press.

Figg, J. and Ross, A. (1981) 'Analysing a school system: a practical exercise', in B. Gillham (ed.) *Problem Behaviour in the Secondary School*. Beckenham: Croom Helm.

Fish, J. (Chairman) (1985) *Educational Opportunities for All?* ILEA.

Fish, J. (1985) *Special Education: The Way Ahead*. Milton Keynes: Open University Press.

Galton, M. and Simon, B. (eds) (1980) *Progress and Performance in the Primary Classroom*. London: Routledge and Kegan Paul.

Galton, M., Simon, B. and Croll, P. (1980) *Inside the Primary Classroom*. London: Routledge and Kegan Paul.

George, A. (1984) *Resource-Based Learning for School Governors*. Beckenham: Croom Helm.

Gipps, C. and Gross, H. (1985) 'Do teachers have special needs too?' Occasional Paper No. 5, *Screening and Special Educational Needs in Schools Project*. Institute of Education, London University.

Gliedman, J. and Roth, W. (1981) 'Parents and professionals', in W. Swann (ed.) *The Practice of Special Education*. Oxford: Basil Blackwell and Open University Press.

Hallmark, N. (1983) 'A support service to primary schools', in A. Booth and P. Potts (eds) *Integrating Special Education*. Oxford: Basil Blackwell.

Hallmark, N. and Dessent, A. (1982) A special education service centre, *British Journal of Special Education*, **9** (1).

Hart, S. (1986) In-class support teaching: tackling Fish, *British Journal of Special Education*, **13** (2), June.

Hegarty, S., Pocklington, K. and Lucas, D. (1982) *Integration in Action: Case studies in the Integration of Pupils with Special Needs*. Windsor: NFER-Nelson.

Hockley, L. (1985) On being a support teacher, *British Journal of Special Education*, **12** (1), March.

Hodgson, A., Clunies-Ross, L. and Hegarty, S. (1984) *Learning Together: Teaching Pupils with Special Educational Needs in the Ordinary School*. Windsor: NFER-Nelson.

McBrien, J. and Weightman, J. (1980) The effect of room management procedures on the engagement of profoundly retarded children, *British Journal of Mental Subnormality*, **26** (1), pp. 38–46.

Moses, D. (1985) The end of isolation: link schemes between ordinary and special schools, *Educational and Child Psychology* **2** (3).

NAGM (National Association of Governors and Managers) (1984) Paper

No. 5 *Governors and Special Educational Needs*.

NAGM (1985) 'Putting it into practice – children with special needs in 1985,' proceedings of a day conference. 81 Rustlings Road, Sheffield. S11 7AB

Open University (1981) *Governing Schools*. Milton Keynes: Open University Press.

Paired Reading Bulletin (1986) No. 2, Spring. Available from Kirklees School Psychological Service, Oldgate House, 2 Oldgate, Huddersfield, West Yorkshire. HD1 6QU.

Potts, P. (1985) 'Training for teamwork', in J. Sayer and N. Jones (eds) *Teacher Training and Special Educational Needs*. Beckenham: Croom Helm.

Quicke, J. (1985) 'Initial teacher education and the role of support agencies', in J. Sayer and N. Jones (eds) op. cit.

Sayer, J. (1985) 'A whole-school approach to meeting all needs', in J. Sayer and N. Jones (eds) op. cit.

Selfe, L. and Gray, P. (1985) Units in ordinary schools – a step forward *British Journal of Special Education* **12** (3), September.

Sigston, A., Kerfoot, S. and Hogg, R. (1986) CLASSIC. Details available from Allan Sigston, Psychology Department, North East London Polytechnic.

Stonier, T. (1982) 'Changes in Western society: educational implications,' in C. Richards (ed.) *New Directions in Primary Education*. Brighton: Falmer Press.

Stratford, R. S. (no date) 'Productivity in the Classroom', Department of Psychology, Southampton University.

Swann, W. (1983) 'Curriculum principles for integration', in A. Booth and P. Potts (eds) *Integrating Special Education*. Oxford: Basil Blackwell.

Thomas, G. (1985) Room management in mainstream education, *Educational Research* **27** (3).

Thomas, G. (1986) Integrating personnel in order to integrate children, *Support for Learning*, **1** (1), February.

Thomas, G. and Jackson, B. (1986) The whole-school approach to integration, *British Journal of Special Education*, **13** (1), March.

Thompson, D. and Arora, T. (1985) What is consistent in the attitudes of teachers to integration? *Educational and Child Psychology* **2** (3).

Thomson, V. (1984) 'Links with other professionals: the head as a multidisciplinary team member', in A. Bowers (ed.) *Management and the Special School*. Beckenham: Croom Helm.

Wolfendale, S. (1983) *Parental Participation in Children's Development and Education*. London: Gordon and Breach Science Publishers.

Wood, J. (1984) *Adapting Instruction for the Mainstream*. Columbus OH: Charles E. Merrill.

6

Staff development and inservice training: encouraging responsibility

At the heart of all debate on alternative and better ways of meeting children's needs within schools is the issue of teachers themselves and what they bring or do not bring to the educational process. Indeed, what they represent, how they are defined and define themselves are lively components of any debate.

Concern with practitioners who have the care and educational responsibility for children in school is, in this book, equal to concern with children themselves. A multifaceted set of perspectives is advanced, of which teachers' training and expertise to deal with the gamut of children in their charge is paramount.

As we have seen from the previous chapter, Alexander (1984) is in no doubt about the immense responsibility placed upon the teacher. It could be argued that few people are in much doubt about that premise, hence the seemingly never-ending stream of pronouncements from the DES, teaching unions, professional associations and training institutions as to what teaching should consist of and what teachers should 'possess' in the way of skills and qualities.

It may not be possible to escape all charges that, by its very existence, the chapter sets out prescriptions. Indeed the purpose of the book, and of this series, may be seen to be directed towards the changing of attitudes and acquiring of skills on the part of its readers. It would be dishonest to pretend that a chapter on the subject of staff development and inservice training could hope to stand austerely apart from the many recipes for effective teaching that are part and parcel of the initial and continuing education of teachers. However, the specific aims of the chapter are as follows:

1. To raise the question of teachers' rights and what have been called the 'special needs of teachers' (Galloway, 1985) within the context of meeting children's needs.
2. To describe some key recent and current developments in inservice education and to demonstrate how these utilise different models.
3. To examine how, within the perspectives of an ecological approach and collective responsibility (particularly as spelled

out in chapter 5), teachers can make self-appraisals of their existing skills and experiences and support each other in continued personal development.

How teachers can manage each other and themselves professionally is therefore one keynote of this chapter.

So emphasis will be placed on positively moving forward on the basis of current scenarios within primary schools rather than on easy invocation of 'teacher-deficit' models. A number of related conceptual issues will be touched upon, for this is an area that cannot lightly be summed into a set of prescriptions.

TEACHER TRAINING AND THE PLACE OF SPECIAL NEEDS

Since the concept of special needs has only been defined and officially used within the last ten years, it does not come as a surprise to discover that earlier textbooks for teachers in initial training do not mention the term. Post-Second World War teacher training might make mention of 'the slower learner' and touched upon remedial teaching; it may have made passing reference to mental and physical handicap. But, as the Warnock report attested, hardly any training courses dealt properly with these elements.

However – and this may be one of the sources of the ambiguity identified and discussed below – attitudes to 'failing' children were, nevertheless, inculcated and shaped during initial teacher training by virtue of the curriculum components of the disciplines of sociology and psychology. Alexander (1984) has drawn attention to a subtle sensitising process that took place as students were introduced to concepts and evidence of inadequate family background, parental attitudes and their effects upon educational attainment. Schools were alleged to be able to 'compensate' for depriving circumstances only up to a point and certainly were absolved from even greater responsibility than that.

So a whole edifice was erected around confused and confusing aetiologies and 'cause and effect' theories. Educational psychologists have faced the dilemma for years as to whether or not to collude with the 'failing parents', 'inadequate home' explanation for educational underachievement and social maladjustment. Their own database has not been secure enough to effectively refute teachers' a priori judgements in this regard.

These remarks are less an indictment on a well-meaning profession than they are intended to sketch in some of the antecedents of the recent and current proliferation of inservice provision for special needs.

Recommendations in the Warnock Report on teacher training for special needs have spawned many local and national initiatives. Yet, in the mid to late 1980s, we are far from having a unified or generally acceptable model of good practice inservice for practising teachers. Perhaps it is too soon, as there is still disagreement over and lack of firsthand knowledge as to how integrated 'education for all' should effectively proceed. To date, changing attitudes and equipping teachers to meet children's special needs are proceeding hand in hand with tentative forays into integrated education within LEAs.

The Warnock Report expressed its dissatisfaction with the piecemeal growth of specialisms within remedial and special education, which for many years came about pragmatically and 'on the job', rather than there being post-experience training corollaries. As far as delivering a unified service was concerned, the Report advocated the local creation of a Special Education Advisory and Support Service. Towards the medium- and longer-term ends of having such a unified service for special needs, which itself would be firmly embedded with integrated provision, the Report went on to consider how best initial and continuing training could develop over the next few years. The Committee's suggestions included a mandatory element in initial teacher training on special education and an available specialist special needs option. For inservice training they advocated short and longer local and accredited courses (pages 355–357 for summary of recommendations).

Many initiatives of the last few years have flowed from these recommendations (see Croll and Moses, 1985, page 153). What is important to note here is that the Warnock Report emphasised, if not the indivisibility between 'special' and 'ordinary', then the centrality of the concept of 'special' needs. The Report firmly places within the class teachers' orbit the responsibility for recognising 'early signs of possible special need … this requires that teachers should know how to identify the signs of special need' (page 55, para 4.18).

Textbooks written explicitly for intending teachers on special needs are sparse (see Sewell, 1986; also Cohen and Cohen, 1986). Even in an exposition on 'collaborative teacher education' (Exeter University, 1986) individual learning needs, the broadest context of 'special' needs are not explored as a valid aspect of these more recent forms of collaborative work between teacher training institutions and schools. Although the editor of the pamphlet affirms that the old demarcations of the four main educational disciplines have gone, he does not suggest what ideology of 'education for all' should inform a model of teacher-training such as IT–INSET (see chapters of Preston and Ashton in the Exeter publication). However, Gulliford (1985) describes the encouraging signs that consideration of special needs is being incorporated into initial training.

PROFESSIONAL DEVELOPMENT AND SPECIAL NEEDS: SOME ISSUES

Contradictions

The nature of the word 'training' is discussed in some books cited in this section and, as we shall see, there is an array of inservice opportunities that encompass qualitative and practical aspects. In the prescriptions and training models that have emanated from the various bodies cited at the outset of the chapter, one can discern an ambiguity. On the one hand, as Warnock says, teachers trained to teach ordinary classes should be equipped to recognise and cope with special needs; on the other hand, special needs are seen as a responsibility for specialists. It is indeed a thin dividing line – the balancing act for LEAs is to ensure adequate inservice training for special needs for 'ordinary' teachers whilst at the same time guaranteeing support to them from specialists, who also have a training agenda. One part of this dilemma is exposed by Sayer (1985) who asks:

> Do we want in any one school or group of schools a distinct body of specific professionals whose sole activity is to be a specialist resource to others or to children with special needs and who therefore lose much of their initial training as 'ordinary' teachers?
> (page 3)

Whose responsibility is it to address the central issue; are the skills and expertise seen to be needed for special needs teaching different from core teaching skills for teaching all children? The question is rhetorical as far as this book is concerned, since it is too vast in scope to be resolved within one chapter. Another inherent issue within special needs inservice is the possible danger of 'deskilling teachers' and leading them 'to believe that only specialists can help children with special needs and that their own pedagogic skills are irrelevant.' (Mongan, 1985, page 45.) So how can teachers best be assisted to feel confident that 'there is no mystique about remedial education nor are its methods intrinsically different from those employed by successful teachers anywhere'? (Gulliford, 1985, page 22 quoting from the Bullock Report.) All that 'successful teachers' have to do, it seems, is to apply 'good teaching in such a way that failure is replaced by a sense of achievement' (Gulliford, op. cit.).

Teachers' rights and teachers' needs

In the haste to heed the clarion call of Warnock and others for expansion of inservice opportunities in special needs, organisers have not always seen discursive elements as paramount, have assumed that educationalists share the aspiration of putting children's interest first. The issue of teachers' rights is seen to be the proper domain of the negotiators who bargain for increased salary and improved working conditions.

To argue by analogy, Pugh and De'Ath (1984) perceived that the needs of children could best be met if the needs of parents were, too. Similarly, it follows that if children are seen to have rights, these can be expressed and realised if their teachers' rights are also acknowledged.

Invoking what they regard as appropriate language, some writers have expressed these rights in terms of 'teachers' special needs'. Gipps and Gross (1985) conclude from their survey

> what this does show is that unless teachers are involved in the developments, feel consulted and communicated with, they will feel dissatisfied and disaffected; teachers do have special needs too.
> (page 28)

Galloway devotes a chapter to the 'special educational needs of teachers' and reviews the notions of stress and satisfaction in teaching with particular reference to special needs. He is of the opinion that it is a 'neglected aspect of special educational needs, namely the effect of the school's climate on its teachers as well as on its pupils' (page 158). The budding literature on teacher stress in the United Kingdom (Gray and Freeman, in press) is one manifestation of the growing view that teachers have the right to have their own professional needs met.

Maybe one requisite of local inservice ought to be an exercise early during a course on self and group identification of what participants perceive their training needs to be, within the aims and objectives of the particular course. This activity could generate further identification of their rights *vis-à-vis* the broader context of their LEA policy and provision for special needs.

Teaching qualities

It is a bold person who attempts to define what a 'good' teacher is and braves accusations of 'value-judgements'. Haysom (in the Exeter University pamphlet, 1986) reflects, after years spent in education, that 'the qualities or characteristics of good teaching cannot be defined' (page 30). Yet the DES has the temerity to do just that (1985). In a paragraph entitled 'qualities of good teachers' the reader is treated to a number of characteristics that make up the good teacher. These are reminiscent of pulpit-thumping sermons to 'be reliable, punctual, co-operative', 'willing to take on essential tasks which relate to the care and safety of those in their charge', 'they are of such a personality and character that they are able to command the respect of their pupils', 'their genuine interest and curiosity about what pupils say and think and the quality of their professional concern for individuals' (pages 2 and 3). The DES sees fit to list the ingredients for the meal but leaves the making and consumption to others.

Patricia Broadhead is attempting to substantiate or refute firsthand some of the underlying assumptions of various DES publications, of which that of 1985, quoted above, is but one example. Positing the DES statements of 'good teaching' and 'an ideal state', Broadhead is exploring what individual teachers think about teaching. She then hopes to put forward an empirically-based model of good teaching practice.

The attributes of good teaching have clear implications for all teachers, who presumably hold an ideal picture and aspire to act like that ideal, even if in reality they do not. But we might be on dangerous ground if we thought it worth pursuing what the teaching qualities should be of 'special needs' teachers as distinct from mainstream teachers. Surveys are reported by Wood (1984) into teachers' attitudes in the United States regarding desirable attributes for mainstream and special educators. The checklists thus generated reveal, perhaps unsurprisingly, few differences. Wood cites Crisci who identifies nine major categories of skills for both regular and special educations. These are: (i) assessment, (ii) diagnosis; (iii) prescription; (iv) analysis; (v) behaviour management; (vi) motivation; (vii) communication; (viii) evaluation; (ix) human relations. They seem to be a mixture of nebulous 'fuzzy' qualities and more easily categorisable sets of specific skills. How inservice education on special and all needs presents, juxtaposes and reconciles all these necessary components that appear to go to make up the good teacher is a feature of developing provision. These three issues are but several of the various conceptual, ideological matters that underlie special needs inservice provision. This selection serves to illustrate the continuing debate and dilemmas that accompany, indeed are part of inservice education.

THE SCOPE OF SPECIAL NEEDS INSERVICE TRAINING

This section is a precursor to the following section on INSET initiatives and introduces the what (content), how (mode), where (location), and when (timing) decisions that have to be made by personnel, mostly within LEAs, who are charged with the responsibility for organising and perhaps participating in INSET. These include advisers/inspectors, educational psychologists, teachers' or resource centre wardens/teachers in charge.

Adams (1986) criticises the status quo in these words:

> many (teachers) are ill-equipped to ensure that such needs are met. Some may have teaching qualifications but no specialist training for special needs; others may have specialist training but have not worked with pupils across the full ability range. The patterns of training must now be organised so as to prepare teachers more fully for their role in respect of pupils with special educational needs.
> (page 124)

He goes on to specify a number of possible ways in which local and regional inservice could be organised and sets out explicitly the responsibilities in this regard of the LEA, HMI, and the DES and training institutions. These responsibilities devolve directly back onto schools 'the head teacher of every school needs to be able to assume a full responsibility for ensuring that special educational needs are met' (page 126). Adams and his colleagues speculate about the future – 'further development will come as our collective awareness of the needs of pupils, students and those who teach them increases' (page 133). But the broadest context of all is not ignored by them:

> The need to engage the staff of mainstream schools in intensive and worthwhile in-service work in order to equip them to cope with children with special needs is of paramount importance and as yet has received scant attention even within those authorities with a high commitment to integration.
> (page 88)

The summary in table 6.1 of inservice possibilities is based on current practice, and the examples given are illustrative and in no way intended to be inclusive or suggestive.

Implied in this listing are any number or combination of aims and course objectives. What should also be included as an integral planning consideration is the relationship between inservice and continued development work once a course participant is back at base. For example, does inservice set in motion consequent self-development and further work maintained by associated interest and motivation?

Table 6.1 *The pattern and scope of special needs inservice*

Content	Introduction to special needs for class teachers and/or newly-appointed special needs posts, covering:

Content | Introduction to special needs for class teachers and/or newly-appointed special needs posts, covering:
   (i) awareness raising ⎫ on special and remedial
   (ii) developing knowledge- ⎬ education, provision, curricu-
      base ⎭ lum approaches, work of sup-
                                 port services

Specific focus – finding out more about, for example, curriculum planning, school-based provision, language programmes, handicapping conditions and teaching implications

'How to', for example, design and implement curricula, develop referral and liaison mechanisms, carry out classroom observation

Conceptual and legislative issues, concept of special needs, integration, Education Act 1981, its procedures and ramifications

Skills training in techniques directed towards competence in, for example, assessment, behaviourally-based learning programmes, counselling

Refresher update on any of the issues, techniques

Mode and timing   Full-time attendance, for example, one year, one term; part-time attendance; for example, day release, evening (after-school); series of workshops, for example, weekly; one-day course/conference; one session

Location   University, polytechnic, college; LEA centre; individual school (or combinations of these, reflects model adopted, see text)

INITIATIVES IN INSERVICE TRAINING FOR SPECIAL NEEDS

It is not possible to represent the myriad of local courses taking place all the time. The intention in this section is to highlight major initiatives, some well known, some familiar to only a few people within one locality. They are used as exemplars, as being perhaps bold and imaginative in conception; perhaps all-encompassing, aiming at nothing less than influencing school policy; perhaps attempting to reconcile disparate professional interests. Those that have been singled out represent a particular approach or model. The initiatives described are representative but not inclusive of current developments, with a focus on primary education.

Courses based in academic institutions with accreditation

Distance learning (with local tutorial support)

The seminal and unique course is the 'Special Needs in Education' course (No. E241) at the Open University. Booth (1985) describes the genesis and the thinking behind the course, which has produced over a dozen course books as well as several major free-standing texts, some of which have been referred to in this book since they are invaluable source books for debate and future planning. By 1986 several thousand teachers had taken the course.

One-year full-time or two-year part-time modes

These are courses that lead to a Diploma or Advanced Diploma, or Master's Degree available at present (see Wedell, 1985). As Wedell points out, one of the prime aims of these courses is to provide special needs resource/advisory teachers, mostly to be deployed in schools. The Institute of Education, London University, offers a full-time Diploma in the Psychology of Education of Children with Special Needs, and also offers this course at Master's (MSc) level. Another Diploma in the London area includes the part-time mode Diploma in Professional Studies with a special needs option at the North East London Polytechnic. These courses have their regional counterparts, such as the part- or full-time Advanced Diploma in the Education of Children with Special Educational Needs at West Sussex Institute of Higher Education.

Academic/LEA link course

Norwich and Cowne (1985) describe the innovative one-term course in special needs at the Institute of Education, London University. It serves the London and Home Counties region, and is project-based and school-focussed. Each participant, in co-operation with school colleagues, LEA staff and academic personnel plans an intervention which will take place over a specified time. The emphasis is on context-bound problem definition, analysis and solution. 'Through the course members project the aim to to help each school recognise its responsibilities for the special needs of its pupils' (Norwich and Cowne, page 169) also see Newton and Hill (1985) for a description of a one-term course.

Another example of 'distance' learning, i.e., where teachers in an area use material prepared elsewhere in local sessions with local support staff, is the use of the special needs 'package' of written and audiovisual materials prepared by the DES, which itself runs regional courses in association with LEAs.

Courses, conferences run by professional and voluntary associations

Professional associations that run courses include the National Association for Remedial Education (NARE) and the National Council for Special Education (NCSE). Amongst voluntary organisations that run national, regional and local meetings, sometimes tailor-made (i.e., responding to local need, or a local request) include the Down's Children's Association, MENCAP, the Centre for Studies on Integration in Education, and the Spastics Society, which has run training programmes for years at its Castle Priory centre in Wallingford, Berkshire.

Local, national courses on particular technologies (skills based)

In recent years as coherent 'packages' (blending theory and practice) have been developed, so training in these mostly behaviourally-based programmes has been made available through local and regional networks. These include approaches that have been described elsewhere in this book, such as: EDY (chapter 6), DATAPAC (chapter 3), PORTAGE (chapters 3 and 5), BATPACK (chapter 4). Staff on these courses may be the original developers or locally trained personnel. Other examples include microcomputers and special needs.

LEA-instigated inservice

A considerable amount of LEA inservice on special needs has of course been generated by the advent of the 1981 Education Act and every LEA runs some forms of INSET. Singled out in this section are examples of thorough preplanning of courses targeted at teachers in mainstream schools to sensitise them and to assist them to respond to children's needs. Materials often include a course handbook and back up materials.

Bryans and Levey, in an area of Birmingham, initiated one such course for primary schools. Levey and Mallon (1984) describe the first and subsequent courses for which the broad aims were to:

- disseminate information and skills developed from psychology to as many primary caregivers as possible
- provide advice about individual problems with the minimum of delay.

The course materials mainly comprised a series of booklets and the course evaluation demonstrated its usefulness as perceived by participants.

Another example is from the north-west area of a southern county LEA. There a team comprising advisers, educational psychologists, and administrators put together and ran a course for schools on special educational needs designed to:

- consider procedures in schools for the identification of pupils with special needs
- help to provide an appropriate curriculum for these pupils
- enable early exchange of information between schools (both mainstream and special), support services and administration.

The written materials comprised checklists, flow charts, descriptive materials on learning and behaviour difficulties and an introduction to teaching by objectives.

Two final examples in this section come from two Outer London Boroughs. One planned a course for teachers from primary schools on special educational needs, the principal aims of which were to:

- develop skills, knowledge and resources of an individual teacher in meeting children's special needs in the ordinary school
- encourage the development of effective school policy with regard to children with special educational needs – developing a whole-school approach in line with borough policy on equal opportunities.

The other London borough ran a series of behaviour workshops, which was behaviourally-focussed. Participants were informed at the outset as to the skills they could expect to acquire from these workshops, and were given an accompanying handbook.

Whole-LEA approach

There are at present only a tiny number of LEAs that have a co-ordinated approach to special needs policy, as reflected in a comprehensive, systematically-planned inservice programme. The Coventry Special Needs Action Programme (SNAP), first described in chapter 3, is the best developed to date with a wealth of handbooks, checklists, video materials, and an extensive school-focussed inservice programme. This can be targeted to individual schools, with continuing support directed to those schools. In principle, as well as in practice, the whole programme is a demonstration of collective responsibility. As with PORTAGE, the organisational and managerial components of SNAP are paramount, and SNAP utilises a pyramid model (Muncey and Ainscow, 1983). Muncey (1986) lists the features of SNAP thus:

- early identification
- involvement of all teachers
- practical content
- active learning
- competency-based
- multimedia modules
- tutored by practising teachers
- staff support
- course development and dissemination.

Leeds is another LEA with a centralised approach to special needs provision in the form of awareness raising and skills acquisition. Initially the educational psychologists, advisers and specialist teachers put together a course entitled LISSEN (Leeds inservice for special educational needs) designed to help teachers in:

- identifying children with special educational needs
- describing skills accurately
- devising an appropriate curriculum for children with special needs
- constructing individual programmes and teaching methods
- monitoring progress

LISSEN also aimed to facilitate the exchange of information between the various educational support services and schools. The Handbook for Schools entitled 'Special Educational Needs' makes a cross-reference to LISSEN. The LISSEN courses were run a number of times.

Then, in 1985, the Leeds LEA made a commitment to the development of special needs in mainstream schools via the appointment of approximately 50 primary needs co-ordinators who were to work in and alongside their mainstream colleagues, play a supportive role, and also develop links with parents and support services. They were in receipt of an initial, intensive inservice programme. In 1986 the commitment extended to the appointment of approximately 50 middle and high school co-ordinators with a similar remit. Again, this has been backed up by an initial inservice programme. The middle and high school co-ordinators' courses are run in association with Leeds Polytechnic. The whole initiative is being evaluated concurrently by Leeds University. Here, then, is an example of collaboration.

Multi and interdisciplinary inservice

To date there are few initiatives in this area, although 'straws in the wind' suggest that this is a burgeoning area. The requirements of the

1981 Education Act for multi-professional assessment and multi-disciplinary co-operation in themselves will provide a spur to the evolution of courses on which people from differing professional backgrounds can begin to share their expertise, exchange views, understand each other's perspectives (see chapter 5).

An example of a course designed to be relevant to people from different disciplines and work settings is one on early childhood education at Roehampton Institute of Higher Education. This is a part-time inservice course and includes participants such as teachers, playgroup leaders, and social workers. It leads to an advanced diploma which is validated by Surrey University.

During 1986 several staff members of the Institute of Child Health, University of London, were in receipt of a DHSS grant to design and run an inservice course for professionals from differing backgrounds on the assessment procedure with reference to behavioural and emotional problems. For Phase 1 the course designers (Smith and Bryans, 1986) edited a multidisciplinary Learning Pack that comprised written contributions by the speakers on a seven-session course. The course was evaluated and led to revisions; Phase 2 is planned to run during 1987, without the original speakers and with the course leaders, Jennifer Smith and Trevor Bryans, playing a facilitating role. Again it will be multi-disciplinary and will include parents. In the longer term, the 'distance learning' potential of the package will be explored. Phase 1 participants included personnel from education, health, social services, and voluntary associations.

From their review of inservice provision in the ILEA, the Fish Committee (1985) conclude that 'professionals of one discipline should be introduced to the work of others and whenever possible take part in education and training with others' (page 132, para. 2.11.72).

PROSPECTS FOR SPECIAL NEEDS INSERVICE TRAINING

In one form or another, there is currently a considerable amount of teacher-directed inservice training. It ranges from intensive, school-focussed, precisely targeted 'training' (see summary chart above) to more diffuse, distant, usually commercial influences such as bought packages like TIPS (1985), which are offered on a take it or leave it basis. In between these extremes we can discern a host of other arrangements, of which the above review presents a selection.

Only very recently has there been any explicit call for co-ordination and planning despite the signposts erected by the Warnock Committee. The actual growth of special needs INSET has been phenomenal and, as mentioned earlier, it follows directly on from Warnock recommendations. The Fish Report (1985) sums up the disjointed nature of these developments:

> current arrangements are often diffuse and uncoordinated in the field of special educational needs provision. This is not to criticise the level of resourcing devoted to staff development and in-service education. It is however a fact that because clear policies for meeting special educational needs do not exist, a coherent framework for in-service education in the field is hard to detect.
> (page 129, para. 2.11. 57)

In fact, the portents are positive. The ACSET report has recommendations for the inclusion of special needs within initial teacher training (see Sayer and Jones and their contributors for close examination and discussion of the ACSET proposals). The Government/DES have signalled a clear commitment by including the area of special needs as one of the national priority areas for DES/LEA joint-funded (though in different proportions) inservice in the new funding arrangements operative from 1987 (Mittler, 1986).

As far as models of 'good practice' are concerned, what we have to bear in mind, before we can confidently point to any, is that we need a longer-term perspective and independent evaluation. The process and the product have to be monitored, and the product judged in the light of original aims, objectives and criteria for effectiveness.

There is a little data to hand (Norwich and Cowne, 1985); SNAP is being evaluated and some of the local inservice cited above has been judged by its course designers – in-house evaluation that may neither be replicable nor relevant elsewhere.

One of the few accounts of independent special needs inservice evaluation is given by Sebba (1985) who describes work in hand. This is a three-year, DES funded project, one element of which is to do a follow-up of EDY (see chapter 5) and another element is to evaluate short courses. Table 2 in Sebba's article presents a summary of the content, focus, population, providers, mode, and location of these courses. The evaluation methodology combines qualitative and quantitative approaches.

Several writers have offered guiding principles for special needs inservice training (Gains, 1985; Fish, 1985; Adams, 1986). Wolfendale (1980), having carried out a national survey into the extent of involvement by educational psychologists into local INSET, proposed and described a model for inservice comprising nine stages. The flow chart representation (below) demonstrates, via the loop, how re-appraisal following evaluation is linked back directly to starting points. One limitation of inservice that is planned by LEA personnel with an INSET mandate is that either or both the consumer and participants do not often enough have a hand in prior planning, identifying their own needs and concerns, and formulating the criteria for course effectiveness. The 'top-down' model has been all too evident and in the following section there is an attempt, albeit cursory, to redress the balance.

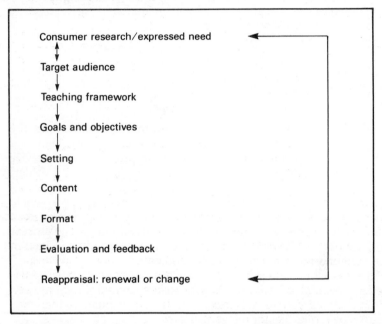

Figure 6.1 Flow-chart illustrating components of an INSET policy programme (Wolfendale 1980, page 52)

TOWARDS A PROGRAMME OF STAFF DEVELOPMENT AND SUPPORT WITHIN SCHOOLS

Some pains have been taken to portray the mosaic that constitutes current special needs inservice training. There are signs of a growing rapprochement between centre and academic-based INSET and the world of schools, with acknowledgements that the valid locus for the development of staff expertise and confidence in meeting needs is in schools themselves.

Within the spirit of collective responsibility espoused in this book there is potential for considerable mutual support by staff encouraging each other to foster awareness, pursue knowledge, acquire skills.

It would be part and parcel of a school policy on special needs (chapter 7) to include staff development; key roles could be ascribed to different members of staff, so that, instead of one member of staff being the recipient of inservice training, taking place elsewhere, various staff are involved in a number of parallel, shared initiatives.

Here are some suggestions:

- preparing and discussing 'case studies' of children in school; using these as exemplars for the evolution of classroom practice, curriculum innovation, how to meet the specific needs of children with sensory or physical disabilities
- setting up a small task force to consider how best to proceed towards functional integration
- staff taking on an assignment to 'job-swap' with special school staff as part of developing working links
- setting up a staff forum for the exchange of ideas and concerns over pertinent professional issues, including résumés of relevant research, thought-provoking articles and books. The forum could invite personnel from other services from time to time. From this 'interface' could flow a number of initiatives such as suggested by Hanko (1985) and which could be seen as part of school-based inservice provision.

Examples are legion. Some of these are already operating, on a small scale within schools, as Hodgson, Clunies-Ross and Hegarty (1984) report. What is advocated here is the creation of a coherent school policy to support these ventures and ensure their viability. The parallel is the earlier call for LEA policy to support the development of coherent inservice programmes.

APPRAISING TEACHING SKILLS

Appraisal of teacher competence and performance is much in the news and has been the subject of much debate in the teaching unions, and between the unions, the government and DES. Whatever formal arrangements are worked out and accepted in the long run, within the realm of meeting children's learning and other needs in primary schools, there is much that can be done, modestly and without upheaval.

Teachers have been only too often demoralised by con exhortations and by charges that they do not possess the skills and attributes (Adams, 1986). The best place to st of self and collective appraisal and skills analysis i now', that is, 'What can we offer at present?', ' currently have?'

This first-stage appraisal, which can be done solo, in pairs or small groups, can then form the basis for the second stage, which is to identify and list what further training and support is needed to do the job or fulfil the role in question. This can be followed by stage 3 appraisal, which is continuing self or group monitoring whilst doing the job/carrying out the role. Stage 4 constitutes review and prospect. This suggested sequence is summarised below.

Stages	Appraisal (self/group)	Phases	Carrying out the job/fulfilling the role
1	Analysis of current competence (experience and skills)	1	Define job or role
2	Identify further training and support needed to do job/role	2	Requirements of job or role
3	Record and monitor progress	3	Carry out job or role
4	Re-appraise skills and competence	4	Review job or role

This suggested series of exercises has been presented intentionally in a sparse, abbreviated fashion in order to suggest but not to prescribe. However, they may look deceptively simple. In practice it would be a demanding and complex set of tasks but worth doing to:

- effect a match between requirements of the job or role and the skills and expertise of the 'doer', and
- promote the confidence of any member of staff who is undertaking a new post or taking on an area of responsibility.

I have been involved in a number of similar training and skills development activities with different groups, comprising teachers, parents and a variety of other professionals who work with children and parents. We have agreed that the initial brainstorming and conceptualisation that form stages 1 and 2 (see above) are not easy. For example, it turns out not to be a straightforward exercise to attempt to categorise one's experience as distinct from specific skills. However, the consensus has generally been that these are worthwhile first steps towards skills analysis, the identification of emerging skills considered necessary to do a particular job, and the training needs for doing that job 'properly' or fulfilling the role.

Braun and Lasher (1978) devote a section of their book to 'role 'efinition' and seek to guide teachers through an appraisal of their 'e *vis-à-vis* special needs children as well as reassure them that current competence is the best springboard from which to proceed to take on different aspects of the job.

An approach to joint/group appraisal and confidence-boosting is advocated by Acton (1984) on the basis of experience. His pamphlet consists of 'know yourself', activities, teamwork discussion exercises, group appraisal of school processes with children, parents, governors, the community, colleagues, and other schools. The purpose of the exercises is summed in these words from the introduction 'to help teachers realise their potential as a team both in holding discussions and making decisions together and carrying out those decisions to the benefit of the curriculum and all the children' (Acton, 1984).

Consistent with a growing consensus that a 'whole-school' approach to special needs must inevitably become common policy and include staff development as an element are management and school review. Recent documents contain suggested questions to ask about continuing staff development, school-based inservice provision, and how the welfare of teachers is to be considered alongside the welfare of children (ILEA, 1982; McMahon et al., 1984; Parsons and Steadman, 1984; Poutney, 1985).

Mongon (1985) firmly put all special needs inservice provision for teachers right into context when he writes 'it should be possible and more profitable to allow teachers to share and contextualise their experiences so they develop a theoretical perspective which illuminates and enhances their own work' (page 44).

This returns us in a full circle to the start of this chapter when the immense responsibility of the teacher towards meeting all needs was acknowledged. The goal of inservice support has to be the devising and execution of the best possible means to enable teachers to exercise their responsibilities confidently, to their own professional satisfaction.

REFERENCES

Acton, A. (1984) 'Working together'. Available from 34 Heaton Road, Stockport, SK4 4JJ.

Adams, F. (ed.) (1986) *Special Education*. Harlow: Longman Publications and Society of Education Officers.

Alexander, R. (1984) *Primary Teaching*. London: Holt, Rinehart and Winston.

Booth, A. (1985) 'In-service training at the O.U.', in J. Sayer and N. Jones (eds) *Teacher Training and Special Educational Needs*. Beckenham: Croom Helm.

Braun, S. and Lasher, M. (1978) *Are You Ready to Mainstream?* Columbus OH: Charles E. Merrill.

Broadhead, P. 'The good teaching project – the practitioners' perspective'. Division of Education, Sheffield University.

Cohen, A. and Cohen, L. (eds) (1986) *Special Educational Needs in the Ordinary School: A Sourcebook for Teachers*, London, Harper Education Series.

Croll, P. and Moses, D. (1985) *One in Five: The Assessment and Incidence of Special Educational Needs*. London: Routledge and Kegan Paul.

DES (1985) *Education Observed 3: Good Teachers*. A paper by H.M. Inspectorate.

Exeter University (1986) *Collaborative Teacher Education*, Perspectives 25. School of Education, Exeter University.

Fish, J. (Chair) (1985) *Educational Opportunities for all?* Report of the Committee reviewing provision to meet special educational needs. ILEA.

Fish, J. (1985) *Special Education: The Way Ahead*. Milton Keynes: Open University Press.

Gains, C. (1985) 'Remedial education: the challenge for trainers', in Smith, C. (ed.) *New Directions for Remedial Education*. Brighton: Falmer Press.

Galloway, D. (1985) *Schools, Pupils and Special Educational Needs*. Beckenham: Croom Helm.

Gipps, C. and Gross, H. (1985) 'Do teachers have special needs too?' Occasional Paper No. 5, *Screening and Special Educational Needs in Schools Project*. Institute of Education, London University.

Gray, H. and Freeman, A. (in press) 'Teaching without stress: a handbook for teachers'. New York: Harper and Row.

Gulliford, R. (1985) 'The teacher's own resources', in C. Smith (ed.) *New Directions in Remedial Education*. Brighton: Falmer Press.

ILEA (1982) *Keeping the School Under Review: The Primary School*.

Hanko, G. (1985) *Special Needs in Ordinary Classrooms*. Oxford: Basil Blackwell.

Hodgson, A., Clunies-Ross, L. and Hegarty, S. (1984) *Learning Together: Teaching Pupils with Special Educational Needs in the Ordinary School*. Windsor: NFER-Nelson.

Levey, M. and Mallon, F. (1984) Support and advisory groups in primary schools, *Journal of the Association of Educational Psychologists*, **6** (4), Summer.

McMahon, A., Bolam, R., Abbot, R. and Holly, P. (1984) *Guidelines for Review and Internal Development in Schools: A Primary Handbook*. York: Longman, Resources Unit/Schools Council Publications.

Mittler, P. (1986) The new look in inservice training, *British Journal of Special Education*, **13** (2), June.

Mongon, D. (1985) 'Patterns of delivery and implications for training', in J. Sayer and N. Jones (eds) *Teacher Training and Special Educational Needs*. Beckenham: Croom Helm.

Muncey, J. (1986) 'Meeting special needs in mainstream schools'. Coventry Education Department.

Muncey, J. and Ainscow, M. (1983) Launching SNAP in Coventry, *British Journal of Special Education*, **10** (3), September.

Newton, M. and Hill, D. (1985) Special educational needs in the ordinary school: a new initiative, *Remedial Education*, **20** (4), November.

Norwich, B. and Cowne, E. (1985) Training with a school focus, *British Journal of Special Education* **12** (4), December.

Parsons, C. and Steadman, S. (1984) *It Makes You Think! Stating Aims and Objectives in the Primary School*. York: Longman, Resources Units/ Schools Council publications.

Poutney, G. (1985) *Management in Action*. York: Longman.

Pugh, G. and De'Ath, E. (1984) *The Needs of Parents*. London: Macmillan and National Children's Bureau.

Sayer, J. (1985) 'Training for diversity: the context for change', in J. Sayer and N. Jones (eds) *Teacher Training and Special Educational Needs*. Beckenham: Croom Helm.

Sebba, J. (1985) The development and evaluation of short school focussed courses on special educational needs, *Educational and Child Psychology*, **2** (3).

Sewell, G. (1986) *Coping with Special Needs, A Guide for New Teachers*. Beckenham: Croom Helm.

Smith, J. and Bryans, T. (eds) (1986) *The Assessment (Statementing) of Children with Special Needs with Particular Reference to the Influence of Behavioural and Emotional Problems*, Multi-disciplinary Learning Pack. Institute of Child Health, London University.

TIPS (Teacher Information Pack) (1985). Basingstoke: Macmillan.

Wedell, K. (1985) 'Post-experience training', in J. Sayer and N. Jones (eds) *Teacher Training and Special Educational Needs*. Beckenham: Croom Helm.

Wolfendale, S. (1980) The Educational Psychologist' Contribution to INSET: a survey of trends, *Journal of the Association of Educational Psychologists*, **5** (3), Spring.

Wood, J. (1984) *Adapting Instruction for the Mainstream*. Columbus OH: Charles E. Merrill.

—7—

Determinants of policy and practice in the primary school

This penultimate chapter is the summary chapter, at the end of which the reader, having taken stock, may feel ready to pursue the theme of the final chapter, which is about transition and looking beyond the primary perimeters.

It is hoped to address, in this chapter, some of the core components that could form an articulated policy for meeting children's needs in primary schools. Throughout the book there has been an intentional blurring of the concept of designated 'special' needs that serve a double-bind purpose; a statement of a child's special needs protects that child, whilst at the same time perpetuating his or her separateness from the mainstream.

If we cannot reconcile these fundamental contradictions the provisions and the procedures of the 1981 Education Act may yet be subject to amendment at some future date. How do 'ordinary' primary schools committed to comprehensive education for all come to terms with having to demarcate between ordinary and 'special' provision? How such schools are enabled to work through these (it is hoped) transitional phases towards a viable educational practice that can encompass all the children within their portals without stigma and without creating either élites or ghettos is the major and enduring educational challenge.

We inch painfully towards these ends whilst remaining uncertain of the means. To be true to the spirit of the Education Act 1944 and to Section 2 of the Education Act 1981, which reiterate the principle of integrated education while concurrently working towards the dismantling of the edifices of separated education, taxes all the resources we have at our command.

The initiatives have to be made head-on; we cannot pluck at one or more of the various pernicious practices that appear to have inhibited ways towards the expression of equal opportunities, i.e.,

- entrenched attitudes
- narrowly-conceived societal values
- blinkered training

• ossified practice

and other alleged iniquities.

We have amassed enough information, it could be argued, from earlier pioneering attempts at integration for this data to be our premise for replication of seminal, proven 'experiments'. The literature on the topic, some of it referred to in this volume (and in Hegarty's overview in this series), provides us with the requisites for proceeding to implement in an all-embracing way, practices we have up to now merely tinkered with (Biklen, 1985).

This is not a call for piecemeal, *ad hoc*, implementation by enthusiasts in any one area; it is a plea for action in the two major areas delineated below.

1. For LEAs to produce and publish a timetable for the adoption of an integrated education service that clearly takes account of:

(i)   the role of special schools, where they remain

(ii)   the deployment and proper utilisation of specialist teaching expertise

(iii)   the cost involved in converting and maintaining educational plant

(iv)   the relationship between school staff and that of the support services

(v)   the use of schools as a community resource

(vi)   the continuing needs of staff for inservice training and professional development

(vii)   the need to continuously monitor, evaluate, and review the quality of the provision

(viii) the right of local citizens, as parents, as ratepayers, as workers, to be kept informed, to express their views, to participate in debates and decision making on educational expenditure.

This sounds like a charter – it is an attempt at identifying some of the determinants of an accountable policy for special needs that would be subsumed into an overall policy of local education.

2. For education staff in and outside schools to try out and find viable curriculum and other arrangements that most effectively and evidently meet all children's needs. We cannot any longer afford not to take a 'scientific' view of pedagogy. That is to say, using precedent and the small number of case studies of effective integration as the foundation, further initiatives have to be set in motion on a proper footing, not of trial and error, but with a considerable amount of planning and control of operating factors.

Primary education has rested for a long time on much collective received wisdom (to which the Plowden Report gave expression) about the criteria that constitute 'good' primary practice (Mittler, 1985). Whilst many of these guidelines may be proven precepts passed from one generation of teachers to the next, educationalists must now apply more stringent criteria that are empirically based rather than couched in fuzzy, exhortatory terms (cf. DES 'Education Observed', 'Good Teachers', referred to in chapter 6).

It is hopefully not too pious to say that we owe it to the children in schools that the ways in which classrooms are organised, curricula are planned, teaching staff are deployed, a caring climate is fostered, should be as a result of in depth investigation. We can begin, too, to take advantage of the increase in the range of educational research tools at our disposal – from the use of classical hypothesis – testing studies, to the deployment of qualitative and ethnographic approaches (Hegarty and Evans, 1985). We need hearken back only ten years to the proposals in the Warnock Report itself for research into key areas at local and national levels (para. 18.15, page 322).

The interrelationship and interdependence between educational researchers and policymakers is elaborated by several writers in the volume edited by Harris (1986).

Policy setting within schools has to be appraised within the broader perspectives and prescriptions for action at LEA level. Yet, to date, few LEAs have formulated a written policy on special needs that includes a vision of special needs for the foreseeable future, as well as a timetable towards achieving the goals. Some LEAs adopt a timid approach to integration and paradoxically opt to retain special schools as an interim, phasing out measure – a caution that militates against an inspirational lead being seen to come from the LEA (a case in mind is that of a large Northern county featured in the *Times Educational Supplement* during 1986 as 'planning to integrate'.

A stern message to LEAs about their responsibilities comes from Gipps and Gross (1986) who reported their data on the various models of helping children with special needs in primary classes. Amongst their conclusions were calls for 'massive inservice training programmes' (see chapter 6 of this book), and particularly for teachers to 'feel engaged' and involved in trying out different models and evolving good practice. They go on

> it is unrealistic to expect class teachers to make these changes and improvements without adequate support from the LEA ... given that primary education is about far more than learning to read we believe that it is ill-advised for LEAs not to try to carry the teachers with them in new developments such as these.
> (page 14)

Jean Eckersley has been researching into LEA policy setting for special needs and based on a survey of local metropolitan authorities, produced a draft specimen policy document (Eckersley, 1986). The components of her blueprint include a statement of aims, a list of objectives, a timetable towards achieving these and a number of corollary statements about key areas to review and change, for example, staffing, inservice provision, systems of support. Constructively, Eckersley differentiates between aims achievable in the short term and those that will take longer to achieve. The applicability to individual schools of a borough-wide blueprint becomes evident in such a detailed timetable. Fish (1985) provides a list of eight core principles that can be applied by LEAs and have clear reference onward to the operations of and arrangements within individual schools.

The rest of this chapter will be devoted to possibilities for school-focussed policy setting in a number of key areas.

DETERMINING SCHOOL POLICY ON SPECIAL NEEDS

Perhaps the anxieties aired above relating to what are seen as irreconcilable philosophies are transitory phenomena; we may eventually find the right formula, we may learn how to create learning environments that can help all children to develop and flourish. In the short-term, however, a necessary part of the prescription towards longer-term solutions will be to identify and articulate what special needs exist in mainstream schools. Such an enumeration has never before been undertaken on a large scale. Hence this series. The specific needs of a number of children have probably gone by default through lack of a rational and coherent plan (see chapter 1) and we can at least, during this time of transition, redress that balance.

The areas that will now be examined are perceived to be key components but are not all-inclusive. Thus this chapter is a guideline not a prescription.

Some of these components provide the common underpinning for specific areas that have been examined in previous chapters. It is suggested, as a basis for action, that each of these areas be considered by staff with a view to their inclusion in the school policy. These are:

- Home–school links and parental participation (chapter 2)
- Management of learning (chapter 3)
- Behaviour management (chapter 4)
- Organisation of school, classroom and curriculum (chapter 5)
- Staff development and support (chapter 6)
- Liaison with support services (touched on in each of these chapters).

Each chapter has attempted to identify, even at points to spell out, what the policy-practice formula could be. Such a formula is illustrated in chapter 2 by figure 2.1 and the threefold plan of action on page 30; in chapter 4 by the elements of a code of conduct, on page 76; and in chapter 5 by figure 5.1.

Readers will recall that the plea for collective responsibility has recurred in each chapter. Prefatory remarks at the outset of a policy statment could affirm a commitment to collective responsibility before defining what it means and how it would work in practice.

Figure 7.1, in diagram form, suggests a model for a policy statement. It would be for each school to flesh out, as precisely and concretely as is necessary, in the given situation, how the underpinning common components (no. 3 in the diagram) relate to each major element (no. 2) The relationship between the school and the LEA is demonstrated, and it is implicit that for every identified major element and common component unique to each school, the LEA has a corresponding responsibility.

KEY STAFF

Within collective responsibility, staff members will have designated areas for which they are responsible and accountable. Some aspects of this were touched on in the previous chapter and, in particular, what some may see to be the central role of the special needs co-ordinator. However, what is specifically meant by 'key' staff members may not be synonymous with the overall brief of the co-ordinators' role.

What is proposed here is that for any child deemed at any time as having special needs; needing a planned programme; needing access to certain resources – will have allocated one key member of staff, or key worker, to act as prime reference point, as main liaison, and who may, too, accept responsibility for the execution of curriculum and other arrangements. In other words, the key staff member undertakes to 'manage' the special needs programme for that child and to initiate reviews. There is considerable local case study evidence that the absence of key workers can increase the risk of children slipping through various networks.

Certainly the key worker can also be the special needs co-ordinator, and this may be an aspect of the role that evolves (Churcher, 1985; Hanko, 1985). On the other hand, the decision as to who is best placed to act as key worker for a particular child will need to take account of that child's unique and current

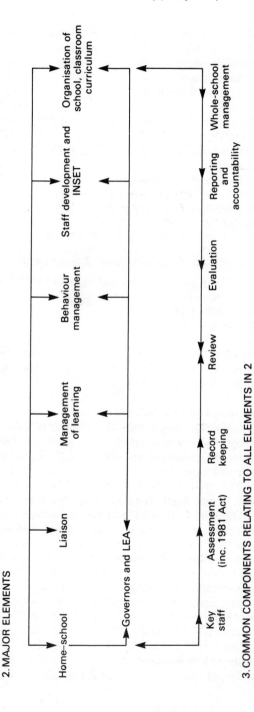

1. AFFIRMATION AND COMMITMENT
· definition of special needs
· collective responsibility
· code of conduct

2. MAJOR ELEMENTS

Home–school   Liaison   Management of learning   Behaviour management   Staff development and INSET   Organisation of school, classroom curriculum

Governors and LEA

3. COMMON COMPONENTS RELATING TO ALL ELEMENTS IN 2

Key staff   Assessment (inc. 1981 Act)   Record keeping   Review   Evaluation   Reporting and accountability   Whole-school management

Figure 7.1 A primary school's policy statement on special needs: a suggested model

circumstances. So the class teacher may be best placed, or an attached or visiting teacher, the head teacher, or deputy; perhaps an education welfare officer, or educational psychologist would be the most suitable person.

The four case study vignettes below illustrate, hypothetically, the assignment of a key worker who appears to be best placed to take on that role in the circumstances. The vignettes also make the point that we do now have a phalanx of highly qualified support staff who should not be regarded as peripheral to schools but who are integrally part of the collective response to children's needs. Each vignette sketches with minimum detail the provision each child currently receives, lists the people involved and briefly explains the logic and rationale behind the choice of key worker in each case.

Case study vignettes illustrating choice of key worker

No. 1 Colin aged 9 years; *hearing-impaired*
Provision: *in unit for hearing-impaired attached to junior school.*
Personnel currently involved:
Class teacher
Visiting advisory teacher for hearing-impaired children (key worker)
Speech therapist at clinic
Teacher with responsibility for language development in the school
Educational psychologist
Parents
Choice of key worker:
The visiting advisory teacher is well placed by virtue of her speciality and expertise; her links with the other services and the school; and the fact that she has worked for 2 years with Colin and his parents, giving advice and support.

No. 2 Fiona aged 10 years; *in receipt of a Statement under the Education Act 1981, with 'moderate learning difficulties'*
Provision: *in junior school, in ordinary class, with curriculum support.*
Personnel currently involved:
Class teacher
Special Needs Co-ordinator (key worker)
Visiting advisory teacher from local special school for moderate learning difficulties
Educational psychologist
Parents
Choice of key worker:
The Special Needs Co-ordinator is well placed for she works closely

with the class teacher and visiting teacher and has visited the latter's school. She has also worked towards involving Fiona's parents in school and home-based programmes. Her home visiting brief is an asset in this situation.

No. 3 Meryl aged 7 years; *with Down's Syndrome*
Provision: *in top infants' class, in a school on the same campus as the junior school. She has 10 hours a week in school from the home-liaison teacher. Reassessment of her needs is taking place.*
Personnel currently involved:
Class teacher (key worker)
Welfare assistant
Peripatetic home liaison teacher
Social worker for mental handicap
Educational psychologist
Parents
Choice of key worker:
In this instance, the class teacher was regarded as being centrally placed, working well with the home liaison teacher and developing a good relationship with Meryl and her parents. She would be the link between infant and junior, should a recommendation for continued integration be made.

No. 4 Rashid aged 8 years; *with physical handicap (spasticity)*
Provision: *in a special school for children with physical handicap and attending local junior school 5 mornings.*
Personnel currently involved:
Class teacher of special school
Class teacher in junior school
Outreach teacher attached to junior school (with responsibility for home–school liaison for ethnic minorities)
Physiotherapist at clinic
Clinical Medical Officer, visits special school
Educational psychologist, visits both schools (key worker)
Parents
Choice of key worker:
It is part of Rashid's Statement of Needs that he should be in receipt of some integrated provision, towards the longer-term goal of going to the Secondary Unit for physically-handicapped pupils on the same site as a comprehensive school. The educational psychologist is seen to have the best links with the unit, school, other services, and parents, and will be involved in the reassessment prior to secondary transfer. His involvement for the past 3 years and his overall knowledge of the situation make him well placed to be the key worker.

There are a number of issues relating to role boundary, lines of communication, the extent of the responsibility that a key worker takes on, or is empowered by others to take on. How viable and feasible in practice the idea of a key worker would be has yet to be determined on a wide scale. The Fish Committee took the notion of a key worker (in a sense of facilitator, enabler, co-ordinator) further to examine the 'named person' concept originally proposed in the Warnock Report. There is no question but that there is increasingly seen to be a need for a role that does approximate to 'key worker', 'named person', 'befriender', and that the constant and underlying feature is that the person in that post acts primarily on behalf of the child and his or her family.

ASSESSMENT AND RECORD-KEEPING

Whatever policy on assessment for special needs is adopted will be part of the school's overall strategies for assessing and monitoring progress and performance. In turn, the schools' approach will be part of the LEAs assessment policy and programme (Gipps et al., 1983). Within the sights of this text, what is of concern is that there should be seen to be a coherent plan in respect of

- continuing record-keeping on the progress of all children
- first-phase record-keeping of concerns over children's progress
- agreed means of data collection (assessment, measuring, observation) and sharing of information at this early stage of concern
- second-phase closer-focussed assessment leading to intervention, further action, e.g., referral onwards
- agreed use of forms of record-keeping to monitor action, progress, outcomes of intervention, decision-making.

Readers will find echoes in this list of Warnock's stages of assessment, and, indeed, this is intentional. The Warnock Committee members, nine years on, would wish that there had been, in these intervening years, a faster take-up and implementation of their rational plan for assessment stages and record-keeping.

It remains an untested hypothesis as to whether or not there would be more, or indeed fewer, referrals for Section 5 assessment if all schools had a tight, functional programme of close monitoring of progress.

This book has attempted to set the scene for the development of assessment, monitoring, and record-keeping procedures in the key areas of management of learning (chapter 3) and behaviour management (chapter 4). In both of those chapters charts were provided for assessment and intervention strategies which show the possible input of the various people involved – teachers, parents, child, psychologists, and others. References were given to help set up comprehensive systems that would include commensurate record-keeping forms.

The key suggestion, first made in chapter 1, elaborated in chapter 3, and picked up once more in chapter 4, is the formulation of a Learning Profile for each child. The concept remains a cornerstone that combines assessment, monitoring of progress and record-keeping. It is deliberately not specified too much, except for the descriptive notes and illustrative case study provided in appendix 1, so that practitioners might evolve their own version of either or both the Learning Profile and a complementary Behaviour Profile – or these could be one and the same as in the original conception, i.e., a composite Child Profile.

Involving parents in assessment

The parental contribution to assessment should now be integral to a school's assessment policy and can take various forms, for example:

- home-based observation and recording in diary or chart form (references in chapters 3 and 4)
- completion of developmental, skills or behaviour checklists, rating scales
- constructing 'My Child at Home' parental profile. This author explored the potential of the parental profile extensively, and the subject was mentioned in chapter 3. Appendix 2 provides Notes for Parents, which can be used by parents and practitioners as a guideline for the creation of a parental profile.

The rationale behind involving parents in assessment is that of 'equivalent expertise' (Wolfendale, 1983, 1985, 1986, also see chapter 2, this book), that is, the pooling and sharing of information by people closely involved with and responsible for any one child. This complementary exercise yields rich information about the different aspects of a child's life and functioning, providing a more accurate database for all concerned (and see appendix 5 for the ecomapping exercises which are consistent with these developments). Appendix 4 contains as a flowchart a sequential outline of joint involvement in assessment demonstrating parallel and related activities by parents and professionals.

Galloway's chapter on assessment (Galloway, 1985) is a useful distillation of the purposes, stages, and mechanics of assessment. He welds his overview onto an appraisal of formal assessments and statementing under the 1981 Education Act, i.e., how these relate to school-based assessment. Much recent LEA inservice training on the Act has sought to demonstrate the relevance of the formal procedures to all schools, to show how the 'educational advice' provided by teachers ought to be based on really detailed prior notes, records and assessment of progress and problems as well as on the concurrent assessment required under the Act.

The message in this section is that a school's probable response to a request for formal assessment really does have to be built into the written policy on special needs. It follows, too, that internal arrangements for statutory annual review of a child in receipt of a statement likewise have to be spelled out as part of that policy. The streamlined execution of collective responsibility comes into its own here, for key tasks can be identified on the part of all involved personnel towards the goal of providing an accurate and detailed review of progress for which all participants accept responsibility.

REVIEW, EVALUATION AND ACCOUNTABILITY

Review of schools' procedures and provision was referred to briefly in the previous chapter within the context of management. Abbott (1986) refers to school-based review and self-evaluation schemes as being nowadays accepted as 'one of the major strategies for achieving school improvement'. Work of the last decade in developing school-based review procedures has, Abbott avers, helped schools to assume responsibility for their own effectiveness that in turn offers a basis for accountability 'which is honest and realistic' (page 3). In his short summary article, Abbott draws on his GRIDS ('Guidelines for Review and Internal Development in Schools'. The project funded by The School Curriculum Development Committee) experience and offers a number of basic principles, indeed requisites, for effective school-based review that can apply to primary, secondary, and special school sectors.

The particular applicability of review procedures to special needs policies in primary schools is bound, at this stage, to be somewhat speculative, for there is little work and therefore little precedent. Indeed, the GRIDS project has only latterly begun to address itself to the special school/special needs area. Galvin (1987) offers a model whereby using GRID's format, provision for behaviour problems within schools can be appraised. Other topics that form part of the special needs area can be appraised by using the GRID's five stages, or any other process model. For example, ways in which the management of learning is organised within the school can be examined through a process that includes reviewing:

- curriculum arrangements for children with identified learning difficulties

- how children with disabilities are assisted and supported in class
- arrangements for inservice and staff development on learning difficulties, curriculum development, professional skills
- available and needed resources, materials, and aids to learning.

The GRIDS' five stages – getting started, initial review; specific review(s); action for development; overview and restart – can be applied as the conceptual framework for the exercise of reviewing the management of learning.

The ILEA booklet, on *Keeping the School under Review, the Primary School*, in common with the secondary and special school companion booklets, has been recently (1982) expanded to include multi-ethnic matters, equal opportunities and the special educational needs of pupils. The booklet's guidelines are presented via a series of questions, divided into sections. Of the seven key questions relating specifically to special educational needs three are selected at random here, just to convey a flavour:

1. What procedures have been established for identifying special educational needs and providing for them?
2. What provision is made by the school for those children who at some time in their school lives manifest special educational needs?
3. What opportunities are there for all children to relate to and empathise with those children who have special needs?

However, some of the other areas dealt with in the booklet have obvious relevance to an all-embracing special needs/equal opportunities policy for primary schools, such as assessment, continuity of record-keeping, the building and environment, curriculum, contact with governors, parents and community. Underpinning these external facets of reviewing and evaluating schools' provision are a number of questions for individual teachers and head teachers to ask of themselves. These have implications for staff development, self and peer appraisal and skills training (see chapter 6). Samples of self-search questions, relevant to the themes of this book are:

- Am I creating a climate of mutual respect within the varied social, cultural, and ethnic differences manifested by the children in my class?
- Do I take time to observe and know the children and to build rapport with each child?
- How successful am I in keeping records of children's development and progress – do these enable me to ensure continuity and progression in the educational experiences I provide for each child?

- What particular strengths and expertise have I as a teacher that could help other colleagues?

McMahon and colleagues (1984) point out that priority setting is one of the first tasks in determining which areas shall be reviewed. With reference to the suggested policy model shown diagrammatically in figure 7.1, given that not all areas can be simultaneously reviewed, it is suggested here that areas for review can be prioritised or rotated. Review and evaluation procedures are amongst the common underpinning components in the diagram.

It is consistent with the rapprochement between primary and special education traditions defined and delineated in chapter 1 that in this chapter there should be a plea for primary educators to broaden principles and practice of evaluation to incorporate the hitherto quite separate and distinctive areas of 'special' and 'remedial'.

The slogan 'every teacher is a special needs teacher' is said to be most applicable at the primary stage where a small number of teachers are significant in each child's life. Yet this text has been at pains to demonstrate the insufficiency of invoking that slogan without the creation and maintenance of a whole back-up of LEA-supported and school-based developing expertise, professional confidence, well-considered curriculum, resource, staffing and liaison arrangements.

Evaluation of these practices would seem, nowadays, to be a mandatory part of education. The existence of recent legislative frameworks (e.g., the 1980 and 1981 Education Acts already on the statute book, and the new 1986 Education Act) have strong implications for the duties of LEAs, education committees, and schools' governing bodies. Thomas (1985) points to the purposes of evaluating the many and varied educational activities and considers for whom evaluation is carried out. In a broad-based model of the interrelationship of evaluation and accountability, schools' central place within the locality as a community resource becomes clear. Parents need to see and participate in the opening up of educational processes and exercise their rights for access to information and to be consulted.

One keyword for effective evaluation of educational processes and activities may well be consultation. Alexander remarks (1984) that teachers should participate in evaluation exercises or these become meaningless. Unless the analogy is extended in execution beyond the schools' confines to the broader reaches of parental and community participation, the value of 'checklist' or any other type of evaluation described by Alexander is reduced.

Nuttall (1981) exemplifies a number of evaluation approaches including checklists, starting with an 'outline framework,' and open-ended issues identifying exercises. His examples illustrate the options open to schools in terms of inclusion of 'outside' personnel – LEA officers, advisers, fellow teachers, governors, parents.

As to the 'technical' skills required to undertake review and evaluation, Nuttall gives some pointers. A useful compendium providing frameworks, strategies, and methodology is that of Rodger and Richardson (1985). The five 'areas of concern' identified by Rodger and Richardson are perennial features of school life:

- school climate/ethos
- curriculum
- monitoring of pupil progress
- management of resources
- relationships with the community.

It would be compatible to make a match between those elements identified above in figure 7.1 as comprising a primary school's policy on special needs with these five major enduring features. The successful design and execution of evaluation exercises on any one or more of these features could be a powerful demonstration of true integrated provision – that is, progress of individual children is appraised within the context of appraisal of whole-school processes. By these means the synthesis between primary and special education traditions is seen to be symbiotic and a force for positive change. Rodger and Richardson provide plenty of tasks and practical examples of evaluation exercises. Interestingly they suggest a brainstorming activity using a debating format on the issue of integrated versus segregated education (page 179).

As has already been hinted at above, accountability runs as a thread through all review and evaluation approaches. Much has recently been written on the purposes of accountability and the procedures whereby educational practice is made accountable to children themselves, parents, governors the LEA, and Committees. (Elliott et al., 1981; Hughes, 1985). These writings comprise a number of guiding principles.

Within the area of learning difficulties and objectives-based programmes, Ainscow and Tweddle (1979) proposed a model; but to date these and other proposals remain in embryo, awaiting widespread try-out. Yet the provisions of the 1981 Education Act, including mandatory annual review, statutory 13+ reassessment, and parents' rights to information, to be consulted and included in the procedures are all conducive to models of accountable service delivery in which teachers and others give an account of their work and their results to parents and the public.

Various possible manifestations of accountability by primary schools come to mind within a special needs policy context:

- opening up files and records
- reporting directly to parents
- involving them in assessment (see earlier) and intervention programmes
- reporting to governors
- providing brochures (cf. Education Act 1980) and periodic reports
- holding parent and public meetings.

Being accountable and responsible for the progress of individual children would involve some of the above but can also include contracting. For example, each participant in an intervention programme has a job to do, a timescale within which to do it, and operates within a framework of agreed goals and objectives.

WHOLE-SCHOOL MANAGEMENT

The final common component underpinning the major elements of a primary school's special needs policy (see figure 7.1 above), that of 'whole-school management', has in essence been the substance of this volume. In keeping with the companion foundation book on special educational needs in secondary schools in this series, this book has emphasised throughout, in a number of ways, the import-ance of effective management – that is, the initiation and surveil-lance of change, the orchestration of all the planning, organisation, and execution of those initiatives.

In a book concerned with equalisation of opportunities to fully involve all children within the mainstream of education, devising and carrying out a policy on special needs in primary schools is to be regarded as an expression of human rights. An emphasis has been given to teachers', childrens', and parents' needs, amongst which are granting of rights that have then to be taken up. That schools and LEAs are beginning to take seriously their ethical as well as their pedagogic responsibility in respect of 'needs' is attested in the DES Report *Local Authority Policies for the School Curriculum* (1986). LEA replies demonstrated a general commitment in the education service to the integration of special needs provision into the general structure of education.

A range of initiatives was mentioned:

- inservice training
- appointment of co-ordinators
- advisory teachers

- deployment of teachers with special education qualifications in ordinary schools
- production of special teaching materials.

A policy for meeting special educational needs in primary schools amounts to a Code of Practice for ensuring that children's learning and other needs can and will be met in schools, via a series of statements that reflect unanimity of purpose within a framework of collective responsibility.

From the ILEA's Junior School Project, 12 key factors of effectiveness were identified. These were:

1. Purposeful leadership of the staff by the head teacher.
2. The involvement of the deputy head.
3. The involvement of teachers.
4. Consistency amongst teachers.
5. Structured sessions.
6. Intellectually challenging teaching.
7. Work-centred environment.
8. Limited focus within sessions.
9. Maximum communication between teachers and pupils.
10. Record-keeping.
11. Parental involvement.
12. Positive climate.

The authors (ILEA, 1986) say that, whilst these 12 factors do not constitute a 'recipe' for effective junior schooling, they can provide a framework within which the various partners in the life of the school can operate. They cite as the partners head teacher and staff, parents and pupils, and governors. 'Each of these partners has the capacity to foster the success of the school. When each participant plays a positive role, the result is an effective school' (page 38).

These factors find echoes in the subject matter and content of this book. Let these findings from just one empirically-based study speak volumes for the potential of policy and practice for all children who have needs.

REFERENCES

Abbott, R. (1986) School-based review: plague or panacea? *School Curriculum Development Committee LINK*. Issue 4, Summer term.

Alexander, R. (1984) *Primary Teaching*. London: Holt, Rinehart and Winston.

Biklen, D. (1985) Mainstreaming: from compliance to quality. *Journal of Learning Disabilities*, **18**, pp. 58–61.

Churcher, J. (1985) Special needs in mainstream schools: feet on the ground, not castle in the air, *Remedial Education*, **20** (3), August.

DES (1986) *Local Authority Policies for the School Curriculum*. Report on the Circular 8/83 Review, June.

Eckersley, J. (1986) 'Draft policy statement: suggested ways in which the 1981 Act could be implemented'. City of Wakefield Education Department.

Elliott, J., Bridges, D., Ebbutt, D., Gibson, R. and Nias, J. (1981) *School Accountability*. London: Grant McIntyre.

Fish, J. (1985) *Special Education: The Way Ahead*. Milton Keynes: Open University Press.

Galloway, D. (1985) *Schools, Pupils and Special Educational Needs*. Beckenham: Croom Helm.

Galvin, P. (1987) *Behaviour Management: Levels of Intervention*. Windsor: NFER-Nelson.

Gipps, C. and Gross, H. (1986) 'Children with special needs in primary school: where are we now?' British Educational Research Association Annual Conference, Institute of Education, London University.

Gipps, C., Steadman, S., Blackstone, T. and Stierer, B. (1983) *Testing Children: Standardised Testing in LEAs and Schools*. London: Heinemann.

GRIDS (Guidelines for review and internal development in schools). School Curriculum Development Committee, Newcombe House, 45 Notting Hill Gate, London, W11 3JB.

Hanko, G. (1985) *Special Needs in Ordinary Classrooms*. Oxford: Basil Blackwell.

Harris, J. (ed.) (1986) *Child Psychology in Action: Linking Research and Practice*. Beckenham: Croom Helm.

Hegarty, S. and Evans, P. (eds) (1985) *Research and Evaluation Methods in Special Education: Quantitative and Qualitative Techniques in Case Study Work*. Windsor: NFER-Nelson.

Hughes, M., Ribbins, P., Thomas, H. (eds) (1985) *Managing education – The System and the Institution*. Eastbourne: Holt, Rinehart and Winston.

ILEA (1982) *Keeping the School under Review: The Primary School; The Secondary School; The Special School*. (Three separate pamphlets.)

ILEA (1986) *The Junior School Project*, a summary of the main report, Research and Statistics Branch.

McMahon, A., Bolam, R., Abbott, R. and Holly, P. (1984) *Guidelines for Review and Internal Development in Schools, A Primary Handbook*. York: Longmans Resources Unit. Schools Council Publication.

Mittler, P. (1985) 'Approaches to evaluation for special education: concluding reflections', in S. Hegarty and P. Evans (eds) *Research and Evaluation Methods in Special Education*. Windsor: NFER-Nelson.

Nuttall, D. (1981) *School Self-Evaluation: Accountability with a Human Face*. Schools Council.

Rodger, I. A. and Richardson, J. A. S. (1985) *Self-Evaluation for Primary Schools*. Sevenoaks: Hodder and Stoughton.

Thomas, H. (1985) 'Perspectives on Evaluation', in M. Hughes, P. Ribbins, and H. Thomas (eds) *Managing Education, The System and the Institution*. Eastbourne: Holt, Rinehart and Winston.

Wolfendale, S. (1983) *Parental Participation in Children's Development and Education*. London: Gordon and Breach Science Publishers.

Wolfendale, S. (1985) *Involving Parents in Assessment*. Partnership paper No. 3, National Children's Bureau, June.
Wolfendale, S. (1986) 'Ways of increasing parental involvement in children's development and education', in J. Harris (ed.) *Child Psychology in Action: Linking Research and Practice*. Beckenham: Croom Helm.

Prospects: sharing responsibility for transfer to secondary school

Collective responsibility for special educational needs in primary schools ends, in an executive sense, when children leave behind their primary schooldays to enter secondary school. But the influence of collective responsibility in action will reverberate into the secondary sector. If primary staff have done an effective job of co-ordination and liaison from entry to exit points, then their children stand a better chance of settling into their new milieu.

The adoption of the first/middle/high school model in many LEAs has reflected the unease over the traditional rigid demarcation between primary and secondary sectors and the massive differences in size, organisation, and curriculum. The middle/high school debate properly belongs to an arena other than this book – suffice to say that the movement has constituted an attempt to bridge the artificial developmental divide of primary/secondary and to render more smooth the transition to other stages of education.

The primary/secondary demarcation, however, remains the norm, though few LEAs have a clear-cut, articulated policy for effecting smooth transfer. Educationalists have not yet evolved viable models for handling transfer and for dealing with the personal, emotional, and intellectual challenges each child has to face at this crucial stage.

Not surprisingly, therefore, the child with special needs is even more vulnerable at this critical time. The familiar and supportive struts of school are removed and the child has to face, with minimum support from new teachers, profound readjustment and realignment within an initially alien, even alienating, environment.

The moral responsibility inherent in implementing equal opportunities to ensure access to a broad range of experiences by all children must extend beyond the discreet enclaves of primary/secondary schools to guarantee that children's special needs are met at transfer time. Planned continuity has to be one of the cornerstones of integrated provision. For those children for whom the

LEA maintains a statement of needs, as well as for other children, the provisions, resources, and staffing available in one setting must be equally available in the next.

This short final chapter addresses itself to some of the practical issues and mechanisms of transfer, especially on behalf of children with special educational needs, and raises questions for debate within schools about the broader longer-term areas of responsibility of primary school staff *vis-à-vis* preparing children to attain their life goals.

EFFECTING TRANSFER FROM AND CONTINUITY BETWEEN PRIMARY AND SECONDARY SCHOOLING – PROVIDING GUIDANCE

There are some texts and studies in this relatively neglected area which serve as signposts. Youngman and Lunzer (1977) point out that there was little research in the area prior to their own study, the major British study having been that of Nisbet and Entwhistle (1969). Youngman and Lunzer set out to examine 'the transfer problem' and explored children's attitudes, motivation, anxieties, and adjustment.

Later studies into transfer in these middle years, whether primary to secondary, middle to high schools, have been that of Galton and Willcocks (1984), which was part of the ORACLE study (referred to in chapter 5), and those of Taylor and Garson (1982), Measor and Woods (1984), and Stillman and Maychall (1984).

These studies have been concerned to produce guidelines for staff, based on their findings, to help them effect smooth transfer and ensure continuity. Over the years, the advice has become more specific, away from the general suggestions contained in Youngman and Lunzer, towards concrete suggestions targetted at key staff.

These are intended to be applicable to all children, the frame of reference consistent with truly comprehensive integrated education. Specific guidelines that are particularly relevant to children with designated special educational needs can be abstracted from these universal suggestions to ensure not only the desired continuity – over information-exchange, written and verbal communication, record-keeping, assessment procedures, and parental involvement – but to effect a precise match between meeting needs in the secondary sphere, compatible with practice in the primary sphere.

The HMI series, *Curriculum Matters, No. 2* (DES, 1985) points out that, on the whole, 'schools have been more successful at these transfer points in looking after the pastoral welfare of pupils than in achieving curricular continuity' (page 50). It goes on to remark that continuity of learning may be facilitated in a number of ways. Amongst these are: primary and secondary schools having an appreciation of each others' curriculum aims and objectives, and devising 'effective systems of records' that will include folders of pupils' works. Secondary schools are exhorted to 'try to adopt the exploratory styles of learning which are characteristic of good primary school practice' (page 50).

Smith (1985), on the basis of his case study focussing on the views of parents, offers a set of guidelines consisting of 21 pointers towards establishing effective working relations between home and school, to ensure successful transition and adjustment to secondary school.

An ACE Information sheet has been compiled by teachers and parents at a London comprehensive school that aims to generate discussion on mechanisms for transfer. Specific suggestions are angled at staff in primary and secondary, to parents, and to pupils themselves.

The Thomas Report (1985) looking at primary education within the Inner London Authority noted the Curriculum Partnership Schemes that have been established between some primary and secondary schools. These initiatives include interchanges of teachers for periods of time and shared curriculum programmes. However, concern was expressed by the Thomas Committee as to a perceived basic disparateness between primary and secondary schools whereby primary schools have remained unduly child-centred and secondary schools are predominantly subject-centred. Children's adjustment to secondary school needs to be facilitated by a reconciling of these different traditions and standpoints. So the committee express the view that the case for co-operation and interchange between teachers has to be based on 'the educational requirements of the children' to avoid 'the sudden shift of practice that now worries many parents and children' (page 60).

Not surprisingly, the report on improving secondary schools within the ILEA (Hargreaves, 1984) echoed some of the sentiments expressed in the Thomas Report and recommended that primary head teachers undertake to do the following:

- adhere absolutely to the dates fixed for transferring records to secondary schools
- send on to secondary schools a profile of each child's work, along with records
- encourage teachers to exchange visits to look at organisation and classroom practice
- send to receiving secondary schools their fourth year schemes of work in English and mathematics.

The particular expressed concern of the Hargreaves Committee was the reported deterioration in performance by some pupils upon transferring to secondary school. Their recommendations are, of course, an attempt to forestall possible attainment decline and to maximise performance of all pupils.

The Hargreaves Committee commissioned a study carried out by the ILEA Research and Statistics Branch into parental attitudes of first-year secondary pupils (ILEA, 1984). When the parents (numbering 216 in toto) were asked whether their children had had any problems settling into school, 58 per cent reported no problems. Reported problems were, in the main, to do with bullying, poor discipline, compatibility with teachers, school-work, making friends, school size, and travel.

Whilst the parents in the sample generally did say that they were pleased with their child's progress at secondary school after one year, nevertheless, what must be of concern to primary and secondary teachers alike were the number of reported adjustment problems.

CROSSING THE PERIMETERS FROM PRIMARY TO SECONDARY: SUPPORTING CHILDREN WITH SPECIAL EDUCATIONAL NEEDS

It is not surprising, given the dearth of models of proven good practice for effective transfer procedures, that even less attention has, to date, been paid to the necessary arrangements for assisting children with special educational needs to settle into secondary school.

This is not to decry efforts made at individual level to ensure the smooth transition of children:

- on a statement of needs
- 'referred' for any reason
- in receipt of a learning programme
- in receipt of behavioural intervention
- in receipt of support of any kind.

Individual initiatives will be facilitated, however, and resources better deployed within the framework of agreed mechanisms.

Attention is beginning to be paid to what such mechanisms might be. Within the sprawling and idiosyncratic network of the Inner London Education Authority, thinking has recently focussed on the viability of local clusters of schools, comprising primary, secondary, even possibly a college of further education, and the attached support services (Thomas, 1985).

The Fish Report (1985) considered existing practice within the ILEA, which was a mixture of pockets of 'good practice' (effective working links between primary and secondary) and *ad hoc* arrangements. At worst, primary teachers knew little about the secondary curriculum and arrangements for transferring pupil records were piecemeal. The Fish Report, drawing upon the experience in one division of the ILEA, advocated that all the ten divisions arrange primary/secondary transfer conferences, to enable teachers of fourth year juniors to discuss the special educational needs of their pupils with special needs or support teachers from the secondary school to which the majority of their pupils transfer.

The Fish Report endorses the development of clustering to incorporate into the network of local schools the contribution of related educational services (e.g., peripatetic, advisory, welfare, and psychological), as well as social, medical, and voluntary services. A flow chart on page 258 of the report illustrates the network and its interlinking.

Wedell, who was a member of the Fish Committee, expands upon the idea of clustering (1986), pointing out that forward planning becomes possible within these agreed structures. Within the present conception of attached on- and off-site unit provision, Wedell argues, these can legitimately form part of a cluster and 'in their outreach work, the staff could then be included in the communication system of clusters' (page 48).

There are, then, a number of ways forward. A transfer document, developed by the head of special educational needs in a secondary school in the south west encourages feeder primary school staff to set out, in precise terms:

- the nature of the continuing special need/problem area
- curriculum and other arrangements that have been made to date
- the provision and support that will need to be provided in the secondary school.

This written approach, backed up by visits and meetings could ensure the match mentioned at the beginning of the chapter.

In one of the outer London boroughs, an initiative is under way to trace pupils with special educational needs through primary/secondary school transfer. It is felt that such children, who have been in receipt of intensive help at primary level, may be left relatively unsupported on transition to secondary schools (Sigston and Pinner, 1986). The aim of the survey, via a secondary teachers' questionnaire, is to appraise whether or not the children are coping in secondary schools, what provision and support are available, and to decide upon strategies for intervention and support. It is hoped that the data generated will also identify how, in the future, children can be best prepared for secondary schooling, and illuminate the types of arrangements that are most successful in giving them access to the curriculum.

John Sayer, in the companion volume on secondary schools in this series, discusses, in chapter 2, arrangements for transfer and for bringing about continuity. He writes 'whatever local variation may seem most appropriate, a transfer system should cover curricular continuity, expectations and environment, individual needs, records, and, above all, relationships with pupils and parents'.

ENLISTING PARENTAL SUPPORT: SCHOOLS AND THEIR COMMUNITIES

This reference to parents touches on one of the features of primary/secondary school transfer arrangements that ought to be central. It has been a prime theme of this book, spelled out in chapter 2 and reiterated in each chapter, that an integral part of meeting children's needs is the incorporation of parents into all discussions and decision-making. Wedell, in the article cited above on clusters, makes this explicit: 'it is obvious that the system has also to extend to parents, who must be involved at various levels of decision-making' (page 48).

In previous chapters, a number of key staff were identified, and, in chapter 7, the notion of a key worker who could play a central role in transfer was put forward. Parents form part of the team, as the Case Study vignettes in chapter 7 illustrate. By virtue of their unique knowledge of their child, parents have an incomparable facilitating part to play in ensuring continuity.

Previous chapters (and see appendix 2 and appendix 4) outlined ways in which parents could contribute their own assessment and review of progress to the learning and behaviour profiles prepared in primary schools. The child profile, incorporating up-to-date parental views could form a core part of a transfer document. Working in co-operation with primary and secondary staff parents could also play a part in assisting their children to acclimatise to secondary school.

The broadest ecological context to meeting a child's needs is his or her community and unique family and social culture. The moves towards community education referred to in chapter 2 should, in the longer term, make the transition from one stage of education to the next easier for children, since the philosophy espoused by all educationalists will be a common one and the ultimate aspirations of teachers and parents are shared (Widlake, 1986).

The goal of parents and teachers alike to reduce any risk of children retreating into 'marginality' (see chapter 2 and Wolfendale, 1983) applies as much at primary stages as it does at secondary stages. A key way of combatting children's anxieties as they enter the seemingly daunting territory of secondary school includes parents and teachers alike:

- talking with their children about longer-term hopes, ambitions and fears
- helping them formulate some (provisional) life goals
- exploring with them possibilities and options available in secondary school and beyond to acquire life-skills and competence in coping
- helping prepare them for eventual adult citizenship.

Such responsibilities cannot remain the province of secondary staff. In an age when profound changes to the concept of schooling itself are envisaged, and the advent of technology renders obsolete some long-cherished practices to do with transmitting knowledge and skills to our young (Stonier, 1982; Widlake, 1985; also see chapter 12 of Hegarty's overview book to this series), teachers in secondary schools need the backing and co-operation of their primary counterparts. Such solidarity could provide a firm foundation from which to plan to meet children's universal and unique needs.

REFERENCES

ACE (Advisory Centre for Education) (no date) *Transfer from Primary to Secondary School, Information Sheet*. 18, Victoria Park Square London E2 9PB.
DES (1985) *The Curriculum from 5–16, Curriculum Matters No. 2*. An HMI series. London: HMSO.
Fish, J. (Chair) (1985) *Educational Opportunities for All?* Report of the Committee reviewing provision to meet special educational needs. ILEA.
Galton, M. and Willcocks, J. (1984) *Moving from the Primary Classroom*. London: Routledge and Kegan Paul.
Hargreaves, D. (Chair) (1984) *Improving Secondary Schools*. Report of the Committee on the Curriculum and Organisation of Secondary Schools. ILEA, March.
ILEA (1984) *Improving Secondary Schools; Research Studies*. London: Research and Statistics Branch, ILEA.
Measor, L. and Woods, P. (1984) *Changing Schools*. Milton Keynes: Open University Press.
Nisbet, J. D. and Entwhistle, N. J. (1969) *The Transition to Secondary Schooling*. London: University of London Press.

Sigston, A. and Pinner, J. (1986) *Children in Transition: Tracing Pupils with Special Educational Needs Through the Primary/Secondary Transfer.* London Borough of Waltham Forest School Psychological Service.

Smith, J. (1985) *Transferring to Secondary School.* Home and School Publication, 81, Rustlings Road, Sheffield S11 7AB.

Stillman, A. and Maychall, K. (1984) *School to School.* Windsor: NFER-Nelson.

Stonier, T. (1982) 'Changes in Western society: educational implications', in C. Richards (ed.) *New Directions in Primary Education.* Brighton: Falmer Press.

Taylor, M. and Garson, Y. (1982) *Schooling in the Middle Years.* Trentham Books.

Thomas, N. (Chairman) (1985) *Improving Primary Schools*, Report of the Committee on Primary Education. London: ILEA.

Wedell, K. (1986) Effective clusters. *Times Educational Supplement,* 19 September.

Widlake, P. (1985) 'Beyond the Sabre-toothed curriculum', in C. Smith (ed.) *New Directions in Remedial Education.* Brighton: Falmer Press.

Widlake, P. (1986) *Reducing Educational Disadvantage.* Milton Keynes: Open University Press.

Wolfendale, S. (1983) *Parental Participation in Children's Development and Education.* London: Gordon and Breach Science Publishers.

Youngman, M. B. and Lunzer, E. A. (1977) *Adjustment to Secondary Schooling.* Nottingham: Nottingham University School of Education.

Appendices

Appendix 1
Learning profile and profile analysis

PROFILE ANALYSIS OF KENNY, AGED 9 YEARS 8 MONTHS, REFERRED FOR 'FAILURE TO LEARN' AND 'IMMATURITY' (23.11.83)

Specific difficulties with learning and behaviour

Teacher	Sees him as not interested and not making progress with reading and number.
Parents	See him as switched off reading, interested in tables.
EP	Does not know letter sounds, cannot synthesise when given sounds, appears lethargic and switched off school.

Positive features of learning and behaviour

Father	Kenny works hard at tables at home with him and builds intricate models.
EP	Likes drawing, is good at it and enjoyed the WISC-R performance tests and then opened up and began to chat.

Learning and behaviour needs

At home	Comics, newspaper stories to hear about and discuss. Home reading scheme: 5–10 mins only, no comment on failures and praise for success.
School	'Tell-a-story' style approach to reading (thorough grounding in story so that he can predict what is coming, was above average on sequencing sub-test). Teacher to show an interest in drawing and model making skills.
Baseline measures	Neale reading age 6:0, comprehension age 6:8

Trends (2.3.83)

At school	Lively, enjoys reading own book.
Teacher	Interested in reading for meaning approach.
Problems	Kenny very apprehensive about the second Neale test.
	Teacher leaving at Easter. HT wants Kenny to go to Opportunity class.
Further action	Find out if hearing test done and results.
	Discuss Kenny with new Teacher and ELRC.
	Phone parents with feedback of current situation.

Outcomes (6.7.83)

New teacher	Pleased with Kenny's hard work and effort.
Hearing	Test done, no problem evident at that time.
Parents	Adamant that Kenny go to Opportunity class as he is still making very slow progress with reading and number work, afraid that he will become a behaviour problem at secondary school, like a cousin, if he cannot cope with reading.

NOTES ACCOMPANYING THE USE OF PROFILE ANALYSIS

To be used for children for whom a programme of intervention has been introduced. It fulfils several functions, and its purpose is described below.

1. It is an overall summary of the child's progress. In this instance it complements and supplements the daily or weekly written records that are features of an objectives-based approach (see 8 below). It aims to provide an all-round picture to supplement specific curriculum-based recording or records used for a behavioural programme.
2. It can be used in conjunction with the (pre-test or pre-programme) initial assessment, but is specifically designed to record *continuing* progress through a programme, and to point to trends in the child's learning behaviour.
3. Hence it provides a temporal perspective that could be an additional aid in enabling the programme planners (psychologist, teacher) to reappraise the content and form, and future direction of the programme.
4. It allows for a balanced appraisal of the child's skills and attainment to be made in that the 'positive' as well as 'negative' aspects of competence are recorded. There is much profes-

sional exhortation to assess children's strengths and weaknesses; in fact there are fewer assessment techniques that bring out the learning/behaviour strengths than emphasise the weaknesses, such that it is not surprising that the deficit model is a tempting one to invoke.

5. The profile analysis approach allows all aspects of competence to be appraised; for it is not an assessment tool, rather it is a conceptualisation of functioning that transcends the recording of specific aspects of performance, whilst drawing on such detailed records as a basis for broader conceptualising to be made.

6. The temporal perspective referred to in 3 can be achieved by positing four dimensions:

   (i) *Specific difficulties with learning/behaviour* These will already have been assessed, and used as the basis for planning intervention. Progress measures will be gauged as the difference between pre-programme learning/behaviour and functioning at the end of the programme. However, these pre- and post-test requirements do not preclude an 'on the spot' estimation during or towards the end of a programme.

   (ii) *Positive features of learning/behaviour* Because a learning/behaviour difficulty is usually the focus of attention, aspects or potential aspects of learning or behaviour that are constructive and could be used to promote overall effective performance are often overlooked. Using this dimension it is possible to draw attention to and record these as evidently present features and also to utilise them in the future.

   (iii) *Learning/behaviour needs* As with (i) these will have been gauged during the initial assessment; however, as the programme proceeds, learning needs may change. Also, a child's motivation, responsiveness and style of learning can alter as a function of the programme (content and teaching method). An additional point to note is that features of learning may only become apparent once a programme is under way, i.e., prior observation and assessment can only reveal a finite amount of information.

   (iv) *Trends* This dimension allows for a transverse appraisal to be made, whereby past and present performance and needs are combined, to effect the making of a prognostic–predictive analysis. In this section the desired/necessary conditions for learning/behaviour can be enumerated as the context or setting for what is perceived to be the likely course of the child's future progress.

7. The profile analysis obtained for any given child can be used, in conjunction with other types of assessment, outcome measures, etc., as a basis for future curriculum planning. One valuable function this approach could serve is to form part of the statementing and review procedures now demanded by the 1981 Education Act.

8. The purpose of the profile analysis approach to recording progress differs from that of record-keeping and charting as used in behavioural objectives and precision-teaching approaches (see 1). Often with a highly sequential, very precise curriculum-focussed programe, the recording is concerned solely and justifiably with the evident behaviour and measurable progress.

9. A profile analysis approach allows for a modicum of analysis based on inference and extrapolation from manifest behaviour, whilst still insisting on rigorously objective use of terms. The statements should be descriptive, impartial and illuminative in terms of summarising present performance and predicting future functioning. Value judgements play no part in this process; therefore the use of a profile analysis approach is a rigorous conceptual exercise.

   Only terms and categories should be invoked that can be operationally defined, but the design is such that there is leeway and scope for the breadth and depth of professional experience to be utilised.

10. *Background and example*

    The idea of this approach to profile analysis was piloted as part of an intervention project carried out in 1979 (Wolfendale, S., and Bryans, T. (1980) Intervening with learning in the infant school, *Remedial Education*, **15** (1)). Quantitative and qualitative pre- and post-test measures were used; measurable gains by the children were recorded. The following examples of the profile analysis of two of the children (JC and SK) convey an impression as to the use of the approach.

The wealth of qualitative data from these forms of illuminative evaluation, sampling a wide range of the children's functioning in conjunction with the standardised test results, enabled us to:

- assess rates of change in performance and progress of the children over the period of time;
- construct comprehensive, diagnostic–prognostic profile analyses for each of the children that could be used as a basis for curriculum planning.

Pre- and post-comparison of the checklists and observation

sheets as well as the trend apparent in the teacher's daily records reveal demonstrable progress made by the children in receptive and expressive language skills, perceptual/motor functioning, learning style, and in spontaneous participation in small group work. The teacher also confirmed that all the children were more settled and responsive in the classroom.

The profile analyses given below as examples, in abbreviated form, of two of the six children illustrate the temporal perspective of the programme as well as the children's progress and development through it. The children's functioning is conceptualised along four dimensions; specific difficulties with learning, positive features of learning, learning needs and trends.

Child JC

Specific difficulties with learning. Lethargic; attentive in short bursts; easily distracted by extraneous happenings; 'shy' and reticent in expressive activities like mime; erratic oral contribution.

Positive features of learning. Can retain information over time, *viz.* story time and Kim's game; can participate in written and oral work with interest; shows evident enjoyment when he comprehends and can cope with the task; in paper and pencil tasks can progress when he takes care; good recall.

Learning needs. Needs training to listen consistently over a period of time; needs training to maintain incentive and application; needs help with sequences of information in description or story making; needs repetition of instruction and basic routines.

Trends. Improvement in last few weeks of the programme in attention; sustained involvement and quality of output. His main problems are erratic attention, easy distractibility, and a tendency towards lethargy. Potentially he is keen, interested, responsive, and delighted at signs of his own success.

Child SK

Specific difficulties with learning. Expressive difficulties, cannot explain or describe; inconsistent listening, 'forgets'; erratic, unpredictable immediate memory and recall; left–right difficulties; rushed learning style in pencil and paper tasks, cannot be over-loaded with too much information.

Positive features of learning. Can be quick and effective at visual association and shape-copying; can perform hand-eye tasks and miming sequences, although responds unpredictably in these; can be observant.

Learning needs. Needs reiteration of instructions throughout a task; needs guidance in constructing sentences to explain or describe; needs training in directionality; needs practice with listening and expressive processes to develop immediate and short-term memory.

Trends. Erratic learning remains; potential interest more evident than before but early 'switch-off' is still apparent; seems aware of his inadequacy; failure is being reinforced by his own performance and other success in the group; potentially responsive.

Appendix 2
Notes for parents: writing a parental profile and reporting on 'My Child at Home'

1. *Introduction* Some parents have had experience of working with and alongside the professionals who teach or look after their children. They have become familiar with completing developmental checklists on their children, reporting upon their children's progress, and having the opportunity to air and share their concerns about their children. These parents have demonstrated how they can effectively match their own knowledge about and insights into their children with the expert knowledge and findings of professional child workers; it is a demonstration of 'equivalent expertise' of each participant in such co-operative ventures.

2. *Contributing to assessment* Parents are *assessing* their children constantly. They *observe* their behaviour, their moods, their worries, their likes and dislikes, their eating habits, sleeping patterns, friendships.

Parents can very often *predict* their children's reactions to people, and events, and can have a good and accurate guess at how their children will behave in a given situation.

Parents can *describe* their children to others, to their friends, and relatives, but also, accurately, to doctors, teachers, and to other people who work with their children.

Parents, with their intimate knowledge of their children, are in the best position to *report* upon their children's behaviour and progress, and to *record*, in writing, as well as orally, and face-to-face, their views, feelings and concerns.

Parents' written accounts of their children can therefore complement teachers' and psychologists' reports and the reports of others who work with children, for example, nursery staff, speech therapists, health visitors, social workers, community workers – and others.

3. *Ways of reporting* This is just a brief list of ways in which parents, working alongside professionals, can observe and record, over a

period of days or weeks, their child's behaviour and progress, preferably with other family members, including the child him or herself, if this is possible.

(i) *Keeping a diary*
This might be a brief daily account of behaviour noting important or significant events, and building up a picture over time of when things happen, how you respond, what concerns you.

(ii) *Keeping an observation chart*
You (with professional help if necessary) could devise a way of recording particular behaviour so that you can see, at a glance, after a few days, or weeks, the pattern of behaviour, what happened before, during and after particular incidents, how you all responded.

These ways (i) and (ii) will also help parents to decide how concerned they are about their child at any given time, how seriously to take any matter, and whether or not to take further action.

(iii) *Developmental checklists*
By ticking or answering yes/no to questions or statements about a child's development in, for example, language, self-help skills, social behaviour, a picture can be built up as to how a child is progressing in each and all these areas.

(iv) *Writing a parental profile on 'My Child at Home'*
Putting together on paper your observations, thoughts and feelings about your child will give you an opportunity to comment on his or her development up to the present, and provide you and any professional with a full and rounded picture or profile of behaviour. Any concerns you may have can be included – but this method also gives parents the opportunity to report upon happy, positive aspects of their children and family life as well.

This information is going to be of vital importance to professionals who see children in out-of-home settings (playgroups, nurseries, schools, units, clinics) since children can behave so differently in different situations.

Until recently, it has not been usual for parents and professionals to exchange information on what children are like in different situations, how they behave in different circumstances, what they are good at in school, at home, and in other places.

Decisions as to how children's educational needs can best be met can now be based on an accurate and up-to-date assessment by parents as well as by professionals.

4. *A checklist of pointers* Here is a list of questions to help you to set about constructing a parental profile of your child at home.

- what would you like professionals (teachers, psychologists, and others) to learn about your child at home?

- what information can you give them that they do not already know?
- how best can you describe the positive, good features of your child at home?
- how can you most accurately describe features of behaviour and development of your child at home that concern you?
- what is the most useful way (useful to you and professionals) of summarising your feelings, your concerns, and your views on the situation, and what you feel would be best for your child?
- can you convey in your profile what your child's own views are on his or her situation?

Finally, a look at the future. It is often necessary for a professional to carry out another test or assessment of a child at a later date, to help estimate whether or not progress in development, learning, behaviour has taken place. To have a parental profile available that can be compared with a later one would be an invaluable part of continuing assessment for everyone, and would, without any doubt, be a really helpful contribution to reviewing a child's progress and for deciding how best his or her educational needs can be met.

Appendix 3
Self-reporting by children

THE WAY I AM

Name .... Date ....
Age .... School ....

What this scale is about

This is a way of helping you to find out more about what you feel
and think about yourself, and to help you decide what are your
strong and your weak points. Also, there may be things you would
like to change in yourself and this scale may help you to decide
whether you want to change any of your behaviour and feelings.
Completing this scale could start you thinking. Be honest – that's
the first way in which you can help yourself.

How to use this scale

The scale consists of a list of feelings and their opposites. The idea is
that you put a tick (√)on the line between two feelings where it
seems to be nearest to the way you think you are. The black dot in
the middle of each line is the middle point and it can help you to
decide where you want to put your tick. It might be helpful to you to
remember that your feelings and opinions about yourself will range
from

always   mostly   sometimes   sometimes   mostly   always

not sure
don't know

Here are four examples to show you how the scale works.

Example 1

No. 1

friendly ✓⏺ unfriendly

Billy sees himself as *always* friendly. He is pleased to find this out about himself.

Example 2

No. 18

reliable ⏺✓unreliable

Janet sees herself as *mostly* unreliable. She would like to change and this scale is useful to help her to change.

Example 3

No. 34

hardworker ⏺✓ lazy

It was not easy for Tom to admit that he is *sometimes* lazy and doesn't work hard at school. He wonders how to change.

Example 4

No. 9

popular ⏺✓ unpopular

Linda thinks that she is *sometimes* popular and would like to become more popular. Perhaps she could think about what to do.

The scale

1. Friendly	—————•—————	Unfriendly
2. Honest	—————•—————	Dishonest
3. Tidy	—————•—————	Untidy
4. Sure	—————•—————	Unsure
5. Lucky	—————•—————	Unlucky
6. Happy	—————•—————	Unhappy
7. Fair	—————•—————	Unfair
8. Quiet	—————•—————	Noisy
9. Popular	—————•—————	Unpopular
10. Kind	—————•—————	Unkind
11. Unselfish	—————•—————	Selfish
12. Cheerful	—————•—————	Sad
13. Generous	—————•—————	Mean
14. Good	—————•—————	Bad
15. Successful	—————•—————	Unsuccessful
16. Clean	—————•—————	Dirty
17. Serious	—————•—————	Joking
18. Reliable	—————•—————	Unreliable
19. Relaxed	—————•—————	Tense
20. Patient	—————•—————	Impatient
21. Helpful	—————•—————	Unhelpful
22. Colourful	—————•—————	Drab
23. Obedient	—————•—————	Disobedient
24. Gentle	—————•—————	Aggressive
25. Careful	—————•—————	Careless
26. Confident	—————•—————	Unconfident
27. Lively	—————•—————	Tired
28. Clever	—————•—————	Dull
29. Polite	—————•—————	Rude
30. Strong	—————•—————	Weak
31. Truthful	—————•—————	Untruthful
32. Sensible	—————•—————	Silly
33. Liked	—————•—————	Disliked
34. Hardworker	—————•—————	Lazy
35. Predictable	—————•—————	Unpredictable
36. Risk-taker	—————•—————	Cautious
37. Leader	—————•—————	Easily led
38. Ambitious	—————•—————	Not ambitious

HOW WE WORK

Please tick a YES or NO for each statement.

THIS SHEET IS ENTIRELY FOR YOU YOURSELF –
TO HELP YOU TO REALISE HOW YOU ARE
GETTING ON IN YOUR SCHOOL WORK

	YES	NO

1. I enjoy doing tests.
2. I always sit at the back of the class where the teacher won't see me.
3. Teachers always say that I must work harder.
4. I never seem to have my books.
5. I like answering questions in class.
6. I look out of the window a lot of the time.
7. I ask the teacher for help if I don't understand.
8. Most lessons are boring.
9. Often I start thinking about other things in class.
10. I always try to get better marks in a test than I did before.
11. I try to make my friends talk to me in class.
12. I take a pride in neat work.
13. I get away with things in class.
14. I forget what the teacher tells me to do.
15. I can't find the time to do my homework properly.
16. I worry about tests.
17. Other boys and girls seem to get me into trouble.
18. I check that I have the right books, pens, pencils, rubber, etc.,
    a) before coming to school
    b) before going to class.
19. I plan my homework a week ahead.
20. I seem to lose a lot of things.
21. I look up the meaning of words I don't understand.
22. I read in my spare time at home.
23. I talk to others about what I have learnt in school.
24. I look back over my work to make sure that it is my best.
25. I only work when the teacher tells me to.
26. When I am in difficulties I ask for help.
27. When I get poor marks I sit down and work out how to improve.
28. My work is spoiled by careless mistakes.
29. If I miss work through absence I try to copy up the notes.
30. I sometimes find reading books in class difficult.

NOW PUT A STAR * BY ANY OF THESE STATEMENTS THAT
YOU FEEL ARE PARTICULARLY IMPORTANT TO YOU. THEN
WRITE ANY ADVICE YOU WOULD GIVE YOURSELF THAT
COULD HELP YOU TO GET ON BETTER WITH YOUR SCHOOL
WORK.

My advice to myself: ....
....
....
....
....
....

Name ....   Date ....
School ....

Appendix 4
'Equivalent expertise': a model for parent–professional partnership in assessment

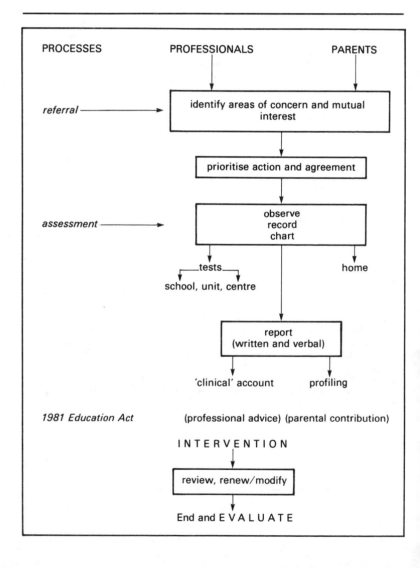

The flow chart outlines the process of parental involvement in assessment within a context of 'equivalent expertise' already referred to (Wolfendale, 1983). It can be seen that the Education Act 1981 assessment procedures are fully compatible with this model that can embrace pre- and post-referral co-operation.

Appendix 5
Ecological intervention and the technique of eco-mapping

Bronfenbrenner (1979) viewed 'ecological intervention' as a way of analysing children's situations. On the basis of such analysis, their situations could be altered and modified. This whole appraisal perceives the child as central in an ecosystem (ecological system). An ecosystem can be drawn up for each child via the technique of conceptual or eco-mapping, that is, schematic representation that enables close as well as distant influences that impinge upon a child to be plotted in relation to their significance. So a diagram can illustrate where and how any child is juxtaposed in relation to school, family, parents' work, friends, the locality, and places visited. In drawing up an ecomap for one child it is possible to represent significant people, for example, parents, siblings, relatives; teachers, social workers, doctors; peers, friends; shopkeepers, youth leaders, and so on.

This representation can also be done retrospectively, to chart significant people and events from the past, in order to consolidate a picture of major past and present influences.

Constructing an ecosystem on behalf of children by means of eco-mapping could be a practical and useful tool. As one technique in the assessment and intervention armoury eco-mapping could serve eight purposes – five general and three more specific:

1. Eco-mapping enables one or more children to be perceived and assessed in relation to a whole class, a year group, a whole school.
2. It enables in and out of school perspectives to be brought together in one ecomap or series of connecting ecomaps.
3. Eco-mapping facilitates and encourages the direct involvement of children and parents in constructing ecomaps, so that what they report and describe firsthand in terms of significant events, places, people is represented on paper.
4. Eco-mapping can be a vehicle for further in-depth exploration of situations, life-events, people, depicted schematically.

5. Information elicited by eco-mapping can be a basis for jointly-agreed action.

These are general purposes for using ecomaps; the ones that follow are specific examples.

6. Eco-mapping exercises can be consistent with applied behavioural analyses or other theoretical frameworks for describing and analysing behaviour since it aims to represent significant influences as reported or perceived (by a child or adult) without interpretation. Therefore, if, for example, *Child A* reports a friendship with *Child B*, this can be represented thus in a class-friendship ecomap:

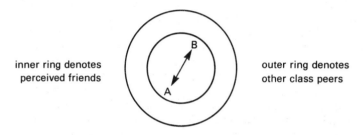

inner ring denotes
perceived friends

outer ring denotes
other class peers

The friendship is neither confirmed, denied, nor explained, merely reported and recorded at this stage. Further analysis can follow.

7. An ecomap is flexible in what it represents and how this representation is made. For example, school can be shown as overlapping with home if, in the child's and adults' view, there is congruence between home and school thus:

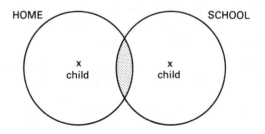

In the interface between home and school shown above, the parent might be a school governor (this would be marked in some way), or the parents might be working with the teacher on a home-reading programme (this, too, would be recorded in some way). Another example demonstrated how size and shapes of ecomaps can confirm the relative importance of people and places in a child's life, *viz.*

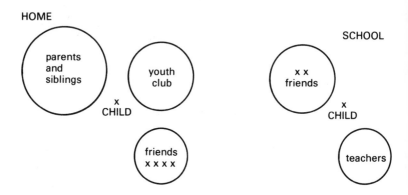

Within the map boundaries, as much detail as is necessary to elaborate and accurately represent the influencing forces in a child's life can be given. The example shown above selectively carries little detail, but further ecomaps can be constructed to magnify and portray influences, people, etc. For example, the *HOME* ecomap shown above with minimal detail can itself generate further ecomaps – like amoeba! So an ecomap can show what forces impinge and impact upon children and evinces to some extent the multidimensional processes inherent in all interaction. Arrows can be used to denote particular relationships and to emphasise how active or dynamic any such interaction is, *viz*:

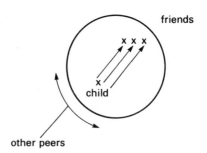

Example A Ecomap of friendship patterns in a classroom

Alternatively, closeness can be represented by concentric circles:

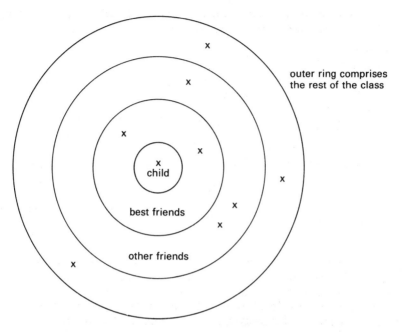

outer ring comprises
the rest of the class

Example B Ecomap of friendship patterns in a classroom

8. An ecomap can be used as a measure of change. That is, one can be drawn up at the outset of investigating a child's situation and again at later points in intervention, or simply, at another point in the child's life.

The potential of eco-mapping and ecosystems as part of overall assessment and intervention approaches has been described at some length because their application could provide further valuable tools in planning and managing for children's learning and other needs in primary schools. Their value could lie in the fact that these techniques provide a bridge between individual assessment (see chapters 3 and 4) and 'whole-school', or systems, assessment, such that children's needs are revealed in juxtaposition with school's provision and contribution of home and the community. Also, as has been stressed, an ecosystem approach is amenable to teamwork.

Ward et al. (1986) describe the applications of eco-mapping or constructing 'life maps' with a group of children aged between 11 and 15 years, who had been identified as needing help in relating to past events in their lives. They were all in residential or foster homes. Since it was felt that children in care often have poor expressive skills, methods of communication were used to encourage self-expression, such as drama and role play, games, and ecomaps. The group members indicated who and what was important to them, using colours to denote how important in their lives were their parents, other family members, pets, and so on. Ward and his colleagues also introduced the related idea of helping the children to use flow chart reconstructions of their lives as they remembered them.

This work has its origins in earlier psychological exploration into topology, concepts of life space, and, of course, has links with sociometry. Readers wishing to explore further the theory and principles underlying ecological approaches are referred to Bronfenbrenner (1979) and to Apter (1982) for expositions on applications of ecological principle to assessment and intervention within education.

REFERENCES

Apter, S. (1982) *Troubled Children, Troubled Systems*. Oxford: Pergamon Press.

Bronfenbrenner, U. (1979) *The Ecology of Human Development, Experiments by Nature and Design*. Cambridge MA: Harvard University Press.

Ward, S., Crawley, J., Hughes, J., Martin, N., and Marsland, A. (1986) Playing Apollo. *Community Care*, 30 October, pp. 15–17.

Name Index

Subject Index